Andrew Dickson White, John Stoughton, Society Religious Tract

Homes and haunts of Luther

Andrew Dickson White, John Stoughton, Society Religious Tract

Homes and haunts of Luther

ISBN/EAN: 9783337258870

Printed in Europe, USA, Canada, Australia, Japan

Cover: Foto ©Lupo / pixelio.de

More available books at **www.hansebooks.com**

Homes and Haunts

OF

Luther.

BY

JOHN STOUGHTON, D.D.,

AUTHOR OF

"*The Spanish Reformers: their Memories and Dwelling-places,*" "*Footprints of the Italian Reformers,*" etc.

New and Revised Edition, with Numerous Illustrations.

LONDON:
THE RELIGIOUS TRACT SOCIETY,
56 Paternoster Row; 65 St. Paul's Churchyard,
and 164 Piccadilly.

A new edition of the "Homes and Haunts of Luther" being called for this year—which is the four hundredth anniversary of the birth of the great German Reformer—I have ventured to add two chapters, and a few paragraphs containing illustrations of his Biography, gathered during German travels since the publication of my first edition. The volume also contains several new engravings, including a fine portrait of Luther, by Albert Dürer, and two fac-similes.

J. S.

August, 1883.

Contents.

		PAGE
I.	INTRODUCTION	1
II.	EISLEBEN, IN SAXONY	5
III.	EISENACH	25
IV.	ERFURT, THE CAPITAL OF OLD THURINGIA	40
V.	ROME, THE PAPAL CITY	61
VI.	HEIDELBERG	68
VII.	BASLE	76
VIII.	THE FREE CITY OF AUGSBURG IN 1518 AND 1530	81
IX.	LEIPZIG IN THE YEAR 1519	95
X.	DIET OF WORMS	109
XI.	THE WARTBURG	136
XII.	SWABIA AND THE BAVARIAN HIGHLANDS	160
XIII.	LUTHER'S JOURNEYS DURING THE PEASANTS' WAR	164
XIV.	MARBURG, ON THE LAHN	178
XV.	COBURG AND SONNEBERG	194
XVI.	THE TOWN AND LEAGUE OF SCHMALKALDEN	218
XVII.	HALLE, IN SAXONY	231
XVIII.	WITTENBERG	238

List of Illustrations.

	PAGE
Portrait of Martin Luther, by L. Cranach	*Frontispiece.*
Statue of Luther in Eisleben	viii
Birth-place of Martin Luther	9
Luther's Father	12
Luther's Mother	13
Nicolaithurm, Eisenach	24
Frau Ursula Cotta shows Hospitality to Young Luther	30
The Luther House, Eisenach	33
Eisenach	37
Erfurt Cathedral, and Church of St. Severus	42
Luther's First Study of the Bible	45
Erfurt	49
Luther, by Albert Dürer	56
The Pantheon, Rome	63
Entrance to Catacombs	65
Heidelberg	69
Luther's House, Neuenheim	74
Augsburg	82
Leipzig Town Hall (Rathhaus)	94
Castle of Pleissenburg	97
Luther at Leipzig	103
City of Worms	112
Luther House at Frankfort	116
Facsimile of the original of "Ein' feste Burg"	120
Luther's Monument at Worms	130

LIST OF ILLUSTRATIONS.

	PAGE
Cathedral at Worms	134
Luthersdenkmal	139
Luther carried off to the Wartburg	141
Chapel in the Wartburg	148
Luther's Study in the Wartburg	151
The Wartburg	157
Luther Preaching to the Peasants	167
View of Marburg	179
Castle of Marburg	183
The Himmelsthor, Nuremberg Castle	195
Grave of Albert Dürer	196
Luther's Lodging at Sonneberg	198
Facsimiles of Indulgences	202, 203
Courtyard of Coburg Castle	212
Castle of Coburg	214
House where Luther drew up the Articles	225
Market Place, Halle	233
The Augustinian Monastery, Wittenberg	241
Luther's Study at Wittenberg	243
Luther's Wife—Katharina von Bora as a Bride	251
Luther's Eating Spoon, used when Travelling	253
Bridal Cup, given to Luther by the University of Wittenberg	253
Luther's Betrothal Ring	254
Enlarged Sketch of Ornamentation on the Betrothal Ring	254
Luther's Wedding Ring, with inscription, " What God hath joined together," &c.	255
Portrait of Frederick of Saxony, by Albert Dürer	269
Town Hall and Stadt kirche, Wittenberg	276
House where Luther died, Eisleben	288
Portrait of the Emperor Charles V.	291

STATUE OF LUTHER IN EISLEBEN.

HOMES AND HAUNTS OF LUTHER.

I.

INTRODUCTION.

IN the little town of Saxe-Weimar, on the skirts of a park round the ducal palace, there stands a plain, straggling, unattractive edifice, with a round tower at the west end. Once a powder magazine, it now serves for a library; and, what is very curious, the spiral staircase which connects one story with another winds round the trunk of an old tree, standing in its original position — its dead roots fastening it to the soil, the green leaves formerly bedecking this son of the forest having been exchanged long ago for a large collection of leaves of another kind. Exploring the book treasures and other curiosities of the Grand Duke, preserved in this unique building, I was conducted by the pleasant and intelligent librarian into a little room, where, in a cabinet, hung side by side a morning robe, a leathern doublet, and a black gown. He pointed to the first as having belonged to Johann Wolfgang von Goethe; the second as worn by Gustavus Adolphus at the battle of Lutzen, with a hole left in it by the fatal bullet; and the third as the dress of Martin Luther when a monk. Three other equally remarkable relics in juxtaposition, perhaps, could nowhere else be found; and their contiguity, at first sight having a hap-hazard look, becomes, upon reflection, harmonious and instructive. For Goethe, Gustavus, and Luther, though unlike in many respects, were connected successively with the march of that spirit of liberty which has pursued its way since the beginning of the sixteenth century— taking a start from Germany, but blessing all Europe, and America as well; and the names just cited mark a triplet of stages in its onward way. The last of the three—the man who wore the morning robe kept in the little cabinet at Weimar—with his universal genius carried the torch of criticism into the chambers of literature and art, and submitted questions, not only of taste, but of reason, to the freest inquiry; and though we may neither adopt his conclusions nor approve his method, we rejoice in that freedom of discussion which he was enabled to exercise—freedom which, in the end, always proves a formidable enemy to error and a staunch friend to truth. Romanism has ever been the foe of freedom; and had Romanism been triumphant in Germany in the seventeenth century, instead of being checked in its designs during the Thirty Years' War, when Gustavus of the leathern doublet appeared as the champion of the persecuted Protestants, the country which gave birth to Goethe, and fostered his genius, would have been mentally enslaved, and free criticism would have been impossible. And was not Gustavus Adolphus the very creation of the movement inaugurated by Martin Luther? A Lutheran by religious profession, he sought to vindicate the cause of the great Reformer, and opened the battle of Lutzen with the grand old Saxon hymn, "Ein' feste Burg ist unser Gott." The Thirty Years' War, with its evil and its good, rose out of the Lutheran Reformation; and freedom in the world, at the present moment, owes no small debt to the mental genius and the moral power of the man who wore the black gown hanging up in the library of Saxe-Weimar.

In the same place was shown, by my good friend the librarian, a Greek Testament, with some of Luther's annotations in the margin; and the veneration and enthusiasm with which the exhibitor referred to both relics were but specimens of that feeling which still exists throughout the Vaterland in connection with the memory of the Wittenberg monk. Not one of the Reformers of our own country has so laid hold of the national mind and heart. Even the honour done to Knox in Scotland is surpassed by the honour done to Luther in Germany. Wherever you go his name is a talisman; its inspiration is breathed over literature scarcely less than over religion. The Teutonic Catholic is proud of him; no town or village associated with the events of his life but is ennobled by the circumstance, and in our time attracts to its precincts more visitors than ever.

Not long after this visit to Saxe-Weimar, whilst pondering Luther's story, and its marvellous influence on mankind, my recollections of places connected with him took shape, and led to a careful reperusal of the histories by D'Aubigné and Waddington, and of the memoirs by Michelet, Sears, and Köstlin. These I compared with Melancthon, Mathesius, and Seckendorf, and then gathered illustrations from Luther's "Table Talk" and letters.

The subject grew, and I determined to revisit some of Luther's haunts, respecting which it appeared to me more information might be gained, and to form an acquaintance with other places where he had lived, but which I had never seen.

Noting place after place where the Reformer had left traces of his footsteps, I was surprised not only at their number, but in some cases at their remoteness from each other. There is no other man of a similar order whose fame touches so many topographical points, and sweeps over so wide a surface. The local reminiscences of Shakespeare and Milton, even taken together, are few, and cluster round a metropolis, a provincial town, and two or three country villages. But how many cities, castles, and homes there are scattered far and wide which may be said to have Martin Luther for their presiding genius! Guide-books call attention to some spot where he went—some fortress and tenement which gave him shelter—some church in which he preached—some locality which his name has made famous; but there are scenes and houses unmentioned in guide-books over which there lingers the spell of his memory. One lights on mementos of Charles V. in divers directions; but even they are fewer, less interesting, and less honoured than those of the humble monk who gave the Emperor so much anxiety, and who by his genius, his faith, his devotion, and his energy inspired the Reformation of the Teutonic Church. Certainly no King, no Kaiser, can vie with him as to the place he occupies in the thoughts of his own people, and indeed of the whole Christian world.

II.

Eisleben, in Saxony.

ON the eastern border of the Harz districts lie the sister towns of Eisleben and Mansfeld. The wooded rocks of the Anhalt duchies, at a distance of some dozen miles here subside into round undulations of arable land, scarcely claiming the name of hills. They bear no comparison with the pine-crowned heights of Rosstrappe and the grassy dells of Alexisbad; yet the scenery in the neighbourhood is pleasant, and between it and the city of Halle, on the banks of the river Saale, may be seen the singular phenomenon of two little lakes close together, the one containing salt water and the other fresh.

As you approach Eisleben by the Nordhausen Railway, the town is discovered in a deep hollow the tips of the church spires and other lofty buildings oddly peeping above the ground; and not until after a long descent over a miserably bad road do you enter the equally rugged streets. There is a choice of hotels between the "Golden Star," the "Golden King," and the "Golden Ship," the latter of which, with an emblazoned high-decker over the door, I chose, without any reason for repenting afterwards. The landlord, a very intelligent as well as civil man, gave the information desired respecting the town, and the particular object of my pilgrimage. There are 14,000 inhabitants, and the extensive mines of silver and copper, with pits of brown coal, afford employment for no less than 7,000 or 8,000 hands, and 700 horses. Here are no manufactories, but there is plenty of trade, and the place is marked by thrift and prosperity. Not very many people visit it except for purposes of business, and of those who come from reverence or curiosity respecting him whose name is identified with Eisleben, the Germans, Danes, Swedes, and Norwegians far outnumber the English and Americans. I told my host that I was in search of localities associated with Martin Luther, whereupon he informed me what I might see in the town; and upon inquiring whether any buildings existed at Mansfeld, about six miles off, connected with the Reformer's school days— for there he began his education—I learned that all vestiges of his abode there, and the school in which he was taught, had been swept away. I was shown two lithographic views of Mansfeld,— one representing it as it is, a small town with a church in the middle, and ruins of a castle on a hill on the right hand, skirted with trees; the other representing it as it was in 1533, when it had three churches, and the castle was in its splendour, with high-roofed buildings and bulbous spires, and walls pierced by numerous windows. The feudal fortress had then given place to the lordly mansion. The old tilt-yard and chapel are still preserved, suggesting pictures of the abode of the Counts of Mansfeld in the sixteenth century. They seem to have been very quarrelsome, and the last visit of Luther to the scene of his boyhood was to compose a feud amongst their Highnesses.

It so happened that a few days after I had been at Eisleben I met with a venerable lady who traces her descent from these ancient Counts, and who keeps up an intimacy with the present remnant of the family. From her I received a tradition to the effect that when Luther was at Mansfeld, only three days before his death, he warned his noble friends against quarrelling and intemperance, repeating these words,—

> " Where the wine flows,
> There the grass grows ; "

intending by this proverbial form of speech to point out the desolating consequences of drunkenness ; " and the prophecy," said my informant, " has been literally fulfilled, for not long ago, when I was at Mansfeld, I saw the grass growing in the castle courts."

When Luther was still an infant his parents went to live at Mansfeld, and having before been a peasant, the father became a miner ; very poor at first, he by industry and management so rose in his sphere of life, that his neighbours elected him a member of the town council. He bought a house and two furnaces, and left behind him above £200 in money. His faith was equal to his diligence, and in his last moments he said to his pastor, " Sir, that must be a poor creature who has not the soul to believe in God and His mercy." It is reported that on account of his skill in the arts of mining he stood high in the estimation of Gunther, Count of Mansfeld.

I had a ramble about the town of Eisleben before commencing my examination of the Luther shrines. It was market day. An open space, girdled by quaint buildings, was crowded with people buying and selling vegetables, the bright colours of which are always agreeable accessories in pictures of foreign life. But not vegetables only ; pigeons, geese, fowls, pigs, all alive and struggling, changed hands after earnest bargain-making ; hardware and divers other articles also were disposed of to numerous customers. There are a good many curious houses in Eisleben, especially in what is called the *Breiter Weg*, one with a Renaissance porch dated 1580, another built in the year 1574, presenting an oriel window full of elaborate ornaments. The subject is the Fall. There are painted figures in relief of Adam and Eve—of God taking the woman from the side of the man—of the tree of knowledge, the serpent coiling round it—and of the guilty pair driven out of Paradise by the avenging angel. The whole composition shows how, at that time in Germany, a taste for religious signs and emblems in domestic architecture still prevailed; and over the door is seen inscribed the noble passage from the Book of Job, "I know that my Redeemer liveth."

Just opposite the church of St. Andrew there stands a dwelling with an ogive arch over the door; the date inscribed is 1500. Luther as a lad might have seen the workmen employed on the scaffolding as they built the walls.

The first object of interest in connection with the Reformer is the house where he was born. It stands at the top of the street which bears his name, and is soon reached on leaving the railway station. The house was partly burnt years ago, and was restored in 1817, but the lower portion inside remains unaltered. It has a modern entrance surmounted by a badly executed bust, enclosed in a frame with the following inscription :—

"In this house Dr. Martin Luther was born, the 10th of November, 1483. God's word is Luther's lore; which abides for evermore."

The building is uninhabited and unfurnished, and at the back of it is a school-house, where I found boys busy with their lessons. The custodian is connected with the school, and he manifested no little interest in the Reformer's story as he led me through the house. I entered a kind of hall with a damp stone pavement, where my attention was directed to some miserable daubs on the walls. To the left is a room containing portraits of Luther and Melancthon; also an older picture of the former, said to have been in the house before the fire. There is another painting, in which he appears in the act of ordination, and there is a wood carving of

BIRTH-PLACE OF MARTIN LUTHER.
(The third house on the right-hand side.)

him and his wife Catherine; in the middle of the room stands a table bearing the figure of a swan, and a small iron box. These are pronounced veritable relics connected with the Reformer; the swan is said to have been the favourite ornament of his study. When these objects had been duly pointed out, my cicerone, in reply to the question, "Is this the room in which Luther was born?" exclaimed emphatically, "Yes, and here in this very corner stood the cradle." Then he proceeded to tell the old story of John and Margaret Luther being on a visit at Eisleben at the time of their son's birth.

The story is rejected by Dr. Merle d'Aubigné, and by Dr. Sears in his memoir of Martin Luther; but there is not sufficient evidence to show that the father and mother were residing in the town at the time of the birth of their distinguished boy. Passages cited by the authors just named are not sufficient to support their conclusion. On the other hand, Seckendorf, citing the authority of the superintendent of Eisenach, upholds the tradition of the parents' visit at the time of the boy's birth. It is remarkable that uncertainty not only hangs over *their* residence at the time, but also over the year of *his* birth, though no doubt attaches as to the day of the month when it occurred. Michelet, in his life of Luther, gives Melancthon as an authority for the story of the parents attending the fair. His words are—"'I have often,' says Melancthon, quoted by Audin, 'asked Margaret at what hour of what day it was her son Martin came into the world. She recollected the hour and the day perfectly, but had forgotten the year. She stated that she was brought to bed on the 10th of November, at eleven o'clock in the evening, at Eisleben, *whither she had gone to buy provisions at the fair that was held every year in that place;* and the child was baptized the next day, after the name of the saint whose festival they were celebrating at the time, St. Martin.'"

If that quotation were accurate it would settle the question, but on consulting Seckendorf, I find in his citation of the passage no words corresponding with those in italics. The statement that Luther's parents were on a visit to Eisleben at the time of holding the fair must be given up, as no fair was held in November.

There is no reason to doubt the tradition that Luther was born

LUTHER'S FATHER.

in the house I visited; but of so large a residence his poor parents could hardly have been possessors. They might, indeed, have had only a part of the dwelling, the rest being occupied by other tenants. But this is an improbable surmise. Whereas it seems likely enough that these honest people might have friends at Eisenach, in a position superior to their own, and occupying a much larger house than they themselves could afford; or they might have had temporary lodgings in the tenement.[1]

There is an old staircase remaining, up which you are conducted to a room where are preserved autograph letters of Luther and Melancthon, two of Luther's rings, medals struck in commemoration

LUTHER'S MOTHER.

of his name and work, and a curious painting of Eisleben in the year 1561, from which it appears how much of the town continues just as it was then.

[1] It seems impossible to decide confidently whether John Luther and his wife were at the time of their son's birth residents in Eisleben or visitors, but I incline to the latter alternative. Certainly they were residents afterwards, at least for a short time.

Close to the house in which he was born is the church in which he was baptized. It is dedicated to St. Peter, and though of no architectural pretension has an arched roof well ribbed and groined. Altogether the structure is in pretty good preservation. Baptized on the day dedicated to St. Martin of Tours, the boy took his name; and the identical stone font used for the purpose remains, the pedestal only having been renewed.

Schlüsselburg states—according to the description of Kœnig's pictorial life of Luther—" he had heard from Luther's relations that his father would often pray aloud and fervently, by the cradle of his boy, that God would grant him His grace; so that bearing in mind his name (*lauter, pure*), he might labour for the propagation of pure doctrine. This bears the mark of a story modified at least by subsequent events, but agrees well with what we know of Hans Luther's character."

Portraits of Hans or John Luther and his wife hang over the church door on the side next to the tenement where the boy first saw the light; and one can fancy the miner with his thin cheeks, and with eyes and nose like his son's, entering the sacred edifice to dedicate to God the babe, of whose marvellous career he little dreamed. Martin received his name the day after his birth; the mother would some short time afterwards have come to the sacred edifice to give thanks for her deliverance, and while engaged in that act might appear to bystanders very much like any market or mining *frau*, whom I had seen just before, passing by in the primitive costume of the locality. Her maiden name had been Margaret Lindemann; and she was a "virtuous, chaste, God-fearing girl," originally a servant at the baths in the town of Möhra, not far from Eisenach; and in the same place lived Hans, her future husband.

When they had removed to Mansfeld, and their child had become a boy fit for school, it was there that he received his education, in some building long since destroyed. It is probably to this period that Luther refers in one of his touching reminiscences, when he speaks of " my good old friend Nicholas Oemler, who more than once carried me in his arms to school and back again when I was a little boy, neither of us then knowing that one brother-in-law was carrying another in his arms." Oemler married one of Martin's sisters.

But Luther's education was still more efficiently carried on amidst the hills and dales, the woods and streams of a pleasant region lying on the edge of the Harz country, into which a boy of his extraordinary enterprise would be sure to penetrate. At fourteen years of age he went to Magdeburg to enjoy higher advantages; and it is said that he and a young companion, named Hans Reinicke, trudged northward with knapsacks on their backs, sticks in their hands, and great tears rolling down their cheeks, to seek a new home and better schooling in the great German city, where, in order to pay for board and lessons, they obtained money by singing chorales under the burghers' windows.

St. Andrew's Church at Eisleben is situated in the middle of the town, near the market-place. It is a Gothic building with three towers, and is externally very uninteresting. There is, however, a mural slab close to one of the doors, representing a family at the foot of the cross, and bearing the date of 1540. This takes us into the last decade of the Reformer's life, and must have been fresh from the workman's chisel a little while before the Reformer's death. The interior was adapted at that time to Lutheran worship, and still remains so. It has a large altar-piece, earlier than the Reformation, in carved wood, painted and gilded, exhibiting Christ and the Virgin. Also it possesses old portraits and new busts of Luther and Melancthon, the latter having been presented to the church either by the late King or by the present Emperor. But the chief object of interest is an old pulpit; it has a sounding-board, and is hung with an embroidered cloth, worked by a Mansfeld Countess in Luther's day;

it also retains an hour-glass on the right hand, to mete out the length of the sermon. In this pulpit Luther preached just before his death. He took his text from Matt. xi. 25—30, and closed with the words, "This and much more may be said from the passage, but I am too weak; here we will stop." The pulpit is used only three times a year, on high festivals. Another just by serves for common occasions.

Immediately opposite to this church is a house bearing this inscription—"In this house Dr. Martin Luther died, the 18th of February, 1546." Of course I knocked at the door and sought admission. A little damsel presently appeared and proceeded to show what was to be seen, and in the performance of her duty was pleasantly loquacious. The entrance hall is large,[1] and the oak timbers of the roof are as old as the house. Beyond in the kitchen and other domestic apartments I observed arched roofs, giving the appearance of something beyond a common residence. A winding staircase of stone, such as you may see in a belfry or a convent, conducts to two rooms, hallowed by the Reformer's last moments. One is a sitting-room, wainscotted all over, but without any furniture. The wainscot has been restored, but the little maid assured me the timbers and the rest of the woodwork were substantially the same as in 1546. It shows good taste and right feeling to leave the room empty, that the visitor may have nothing to distract his thoughts whilst musing upon the scene where Luther received his death-stroke, and paced up and down the floor in extreme pain, uttering pious exclamations, gathered up by admiring biographers.

Here he was with his three sons and Justus Jonas. Here, his host, named Albrecht, and his good wife, waited on him.

---

[1] In the accounts of Luther's last days at Eisleben mention is made of the great hall where the company transacted business and took their meals, as well as of his own private apartment. The hall of the house described may have been originally still larger than it is now.

Hence he went, before his seizure, to preach in St. Andrew's Church, on the fourth, fifth, and sixth Sundays after Epiphany, and to ordain two young ministers, to whom the picture in the room where he was born undoubtedly refers. Here he examined and revised the ecclesiastical regulations just drawn up for the county of Mansfeld by Casper Guttell. Here he also carried on daily conversation with visitors, both friends and strangers, and wrote many letters, of which several are preserved.

Let us copy an extract or two.[1]

From those addressed to his wife—"Dear Catherine, we are terribly annoyed here in one way and another, and would willingly return home, but I think we shall have to remain a week longer." He here alludes to the family quarrels he had come to settle amongst his noble friends, and then goes on to say, "Master Philip Melancthon, you may tell from me, would do well to revise his notes on the Gospel, for he does not seem, in writing them, to have rightly understood why our Lord in the parable called riches thorns. This is the school in which we really learn these things." The riches of the Mansfeld Counts troubled their peace, and pierced them with many sorrows. "The Scripture throughout threatens these thorns with eternal flames; this at once alarms, and gives me patience, for I must exercise my strength in settling this matter by God's help."

To his wife, troubled on his account, he writes again,—"Dear Catherine, thou shouldst read St. John, and what the little catechism says about the confidence we ought to have in God. Thou afflictest thyself as if God were not almighty, and able to raise up ten Dr. Martins if old Dr. Martin were to be drowned in the Saale."

The reference is to perils he had passed through in crossing the river at Halle.

" There is One who takes care of me in His own way better than

[1] The letters quoted in this volume are translated from *Dr. Martin Luther's Briefe* edited by De Wette. Berlin, 1827.

thou and all the angels could ever do. He sits by the side of the almighty Father. Therefore rest in peace. Amen. I had intended this very day to depart in anger," so vexed was he with the business which had brought him to Eisleben, "but the affliction in which I see my native place involved still detains me. Would you believe it? I have become a lawyer. I doubt, however, whether I shall do much good in that line. It is better that I should remain a theologian. It were a great blessing for those people if I could succeed in humbling their pride. They speak and act as if they were gods, but I fear they will become devils if they persevere in their present course, like Lucifer, who was too proud longer to remain in heaven."

Better news followed. "My sweet wife, Catherine Luther von Bora, we hope to come home this week if it please God. God has given us great grace in this business. The Lords have come to an agreement upon all the points in dispute except two or three, and amongst other great ends accomplished is the reconciliation of Count Gebhard and Count Albert. I am to dine with them to-day, and will endeavour before we separate to make them brothers again. The young men are gay, they drive the ladies out in sledges, and make the horse-bells ring merrily." The reference suggests what the appearance of the hills and valleys about Eisleben and Mansfeld must have been that winter. Snow on the ground, ice on the stream, frost in the air, the bright sun shining down upon the country side shrouded in white :—then we hear the clatter of hoofs, the tinkling of bells, and the merry laugh of country lords and ladies. "I send some trout," he genially adds, "trout that Countess Albert has sent me. This lady is full of joy at seeing peace restored to her family. There is a rumour current that the Emperor is advancing to Westphalia, and that the French and the Landgrave are enlisting *lanzknechts*. Let them go on with their news—true or false, it matters little which; we will wait to see what God will do."

These letters were written on the 6th, 7th, and 14th of the month.

The incidents connected with Luther's death are carefully recorded by those who attended on him, and, together with his letters, show his extraordinary activity up to the very close of life. "Shall I be found idle when my Master comes?" asked John Calvin, as he was warned against overwork by those who witnessed his failing strength; and in like manner his German helper and predecessor laboured earnestly in the Lord's vineyard down to the hour when sunset put an end to a long day's toil.

Next to the sitting-room is a sleeping-room, where we are told Dr. Martin died. Like the other room, it remains unfurnished; and here it was that he gave the emphatic "*Yes, yes!*" to the inquiry, "Do you die trusting in Christ and in the doctrine which you have preached?"

More than three centuries have passed away since that great spirit quitted the scenes and employments of earthly existence to enter into the unveiled presence of his blessed Lord; but the transition of that moment when time merged in eternity, and his noblest aspirations and hopes attained accomplishment, seems to reveal itself as one paces the apartment. What makes a visit to Eisleben the more affecting is that the two ends of Luther's life come together in this little mining town. We see him at once entering and leaving a world of work and warfare. The baby sleeping in the cradle at the corner of the room near St. Peter's Church, unconscious of the wonderful life it had begun to live, how near it lies to the weary, struggling, victorious man, full of care, sorrow, and pain, not for himself but others, in the house under the shadow of St. Andrew's!—*there* the streamlet bubbling from the fountain, *here* the river pouring into the sea.

As I walked through the streets the shade of our hero was seen everywhere, and the buildings existing in his time, on which his eyes must often have fallen, became so many mementos of his life and times. One incident is vividly recalled, as related in his "Table Talk." "When I was young it happened that I was taking part in my priest's habit in a procession on Corpus Christi Day at Eisleben. All at once the sight of the holy sacrament, borne by Dr. Staupitz, so terrified me, that I perspired at every pore, and thought I should die with fear. When the procession was over I confessed to Dr. Staupitz, and related what had happened to me. He replied, '*Thy thoughts are not according to Christ—Christ does not terrify, He consoles.*' These words filled me with joy, and were a great relief to my mind." Luther, in his early days, as monk and priest, was superstitious and ignorant, but never careless and indifferent; and in this and many other instances the intensity of his religious sensibilities becomes apparent. Corpus Christi Day was in times before the Reformation, as it is still in Roman Catholic countries, one of the most imposing festivals of the year. No doubt it was marked at Eisleben by a grand procession in the streets, with crosses, banners, candles, and images; priests in richly embroidered vestments, and acolytes draped in white, marched along with slow and solemn step; whilst citizens lined the thoroughfare, and mothers and maidens from tapestried windows looked down upon the grand display. All this reappears as, with Luther's "Table Talk" in remembrance, you wander through the streets of this Saxon town.

There is one more object of interest at Eisleben. On the north side of St. Andrew's Church, and exactly opposite to the house in which Luther died, stands a large, heavy, unpicturesque building, with a Latin inscription over the doorway, indicating its connection with Luther, and stating that it was founded by the Counts of Mansfeld in 1546; and—after being burnt and rebuilt, and then falling into decay,—was restored by Frederic William IV. in 1846.

The fateful edifice is traced back to the sixteenth century, and is found to be one of the gymnasiums which Luther was so anxious to have established for the benefit of his countrymen. His zeal for education was equalled only by his zeal for the purification and prosperity of God's Church. The school, no less than the pulpit and the printing-press, was an instrument in his hands for the reformation of religion and the welfare of human souls. Education had sunk into a deplorable state when Luther was a boy. A little monkish Latin, a little arithmetic, a little music, a little logic, and a little grammar, constituted the common curriculum; and the whole was conducted by ecclesiastics, and by assistants called *bacchantes*—a set of strolling youths candidates for clerical offices, who wandered from place to place to sell for a piece of bread what modicum of knowledge they had been able to obtain. Luther caustically remarked that monks and canons divided pay with the poor schoolmaster, as the beggar did who promised to share equally with the Church the half of what he received, and then gave the outward half of nuts and the inner half of dates for pious uses, consuming the remainder himself. Experience taught him that educational reforms were as much needed in Germany as ecclesiastical ones ; and in 1524 he addressed the Saxon common councils on behalf of new academies. His efforts took effect in his native town, and the flourishing gymnasium within the walls of the building just noticed, supported out of the revenues of a monastery which originally occupied the spot, is the fruit of his wise and far-seeing counsels.

The school seemed to be in good working order,—the youths looked bright and intelligent, the masters were steady at their posts ; and when the hour of tasks and the sounds of song were over, out rushed the strapping boys to gather round the English stranger, who stood outside copying the inscription over the entrance door. The position of the building, near the church where Luther preached, near the house where Luther died, seemed to me most appropriate and significant of his great life mission

—to convert the old, and, better still, to train the young. The Lutheran system of education includes higher and lower schools. The gymnasium is for elder lads; elsewhere in the town of Eisleben I met with seminaries for younger children, boys and girls; very amusing it was to watch them, with satchels on their shoulders, wending their way in the morning before breakfast to begin their work; and as they ran up the steps of the schoolhouse their merry tricks and ringing laugh indicated that the duty awaiting them within, promised pleasure rather than pain.

NICOLAITHURM, EISENACH.

III.

Eisenach.

EISENACH, where Luther went to school after he left Mansfeld, I have visited more than once; and a right pleasant town it is—quaint in its architecture; dreamy, on a summer's day, in its narrow, winding, intersecting streets, full of comfortable-looking German homes and odd little German shops; very spacious in its market-place; very inviting in its hotels and landlords—furnishing, as they do, cosy apartments and wholesome fare; above all, pleasant for situation, the joy of the duchy of Weimar, and the entrance gate to the great forest of Thuringia, which for wooded hills and picturesque towns and villages, in my opinion, stands unrivalled. Of the charming scenery round about the town I shall have more to say hereafter. At present I confine myself to the town.

Leaving the Leipzig line of railway, you enter Eisenach through the oldest building in the neighbourhood, the Nicolaithurm, a gateway having a Roman appearance, which might give rise to divers researches and speculations on the part of an archæological topographer. But we are simply on the track of Martin Luther; so we pass under the shadow of the old arch with only one remark, that through it the boy Martin passed when he was about fifteen years old. We think we see him running along at a brisk pace, humming the tune of a German choral, dressed as a peasant lad, with big dusty shoes, but with a face of no common order—that nose and mouth indicating nobility and decision, and those great eyes revealing far-seeing thoughts and flashing with purest affection—the lofty brow being surmounted by a head of thinnish, crispy hair, which the young urchin, cap in hand, exposes to the freshening breeze. The boy is brave, yet withal just a little shy, for his exuberant spirits have been damped by too severe discipline. "Once," he says, "did my father beat me so sharply, that I fled away from him, and was angry against him, till by diligent endeavour he gained me back." "Once did my mother, for a small nut, beat me till the blood flowed." There was more behind, in the case of this remarkable boy, to account for any depression which weighed down his buoyant soul. From his childhood he was trained so as to turn pale with terror at the name of Christ, for he was taught to think of Him as an angry Judge, sitting on a rainbow, needing to have His wrath pacified by the intercession of the Virgin Mary.

In Eisenach market-place stands St. George's Church, originally a Gothic structure, but now so disfigured that it would be difficult to pronounce to what style of architecture it belongs. The exterior is ugly. The roof is full of dormer windows. Within are four galleries, to provide for which the columns have been mangled in a distressing manner. The roof is hidden by a plaster ceiling. There is an elaborate pulpit, and on the walls are monuments containing portraits in oil, one surmounted by a suit of armour. Nothing indicates the appearance of the church in Luther's time, beyond the barest outline. On two Sundays, in different years, when I worshipped there, congregations of considerable size assembled, but they were not large enough to fill all the pews of the spacious edifice.

To this church, in the sixteenth century, was attached a

parochial school—one of three in the town—for the education of boys, but this was distinguished from the rest by superior advantages for the acquisition of the Latin language. Luther's mother was connected with a family near Eisenach, and by that means he was introduced to this superior place of instruction, where a master named Trebonius, eminent in his profession, imbued his boys with the rudiments of learning, and, not knowing how prophetic his words were, was wont to say, with the pride of a pedagogue, "Among these boys are burgomasters, chancellors, doctors, and magistrates." No doubt within the walls of St. George's Church the lad from Mansfeld often entered when mass was to be said; there he listened, and there he sang, ignorant that he was destined to uproot the Roman Catholic system in his native land, to introduce a plain but touching psalmody throughout its towns and villages, and to inaugurate such preaching as flows from the lips of evangelical clergymen in gowns and bands, so unlike the gorgeously apparelled priests whom he reverenced profoundly in his schoolboy days.

Martin had a good voice, and loved singing. It was the fashion in those days for boys to wander about the country entertaining, perhaps annoying, quiet people with their shrill and oftentimes not tuneful voices. Before our young friend came to Eisenach he was wont to exercise his vocal gifts in the usual way. At Christmas-time he would with other lads go the round of the village homesteads singing Bethlehem carols. One day they came to the hut of a peasant, who shouted, "Where are you, boys?" at the same time stepping out of his door with German sausages in his hand. The choristers were so terrified that they scampered off; and Luther mentions the incident to illustrate the terror which crushed the souls of poor little fellows when he was young.

Martin was poor—very poor. Afterwards, indeed, as already mentioned, his father attained to a superior position, and became a magistrate of the town of Mansfeld; but in these earlier days he was a hard-working miner, delving for ore; his wife being such a drudge as to carry fagots of wood on her shoulders. Martin often talked of this when he had attained to eminence, as great men are wont to talk of a humble origin, if God has raised them in the world. There can be no more contemptible mark of littleness than a vain endeavour to hide from the world early lowliness and poverty; the lower the ground, the nobler the leap which springs above it.

"I have been," says Luther, "a beggar of crumbs, and have taken my bread at the door, especially in Eisenach, my favourite town. . . . Though I have been a beggar of bread, I have prospered so far forth with the pen, that I would not exchange my art for all the wealth of the Turkish empire. . . . Yet I should not have attained thereunto, had I not gone to school and given myself to the business of writing. Therefore," he adds, "doubt not to put your boy to study; and if he must needs beg his bread, you nevertheless give unto God a noble piece of timber, whereof He will carve a great man."

Singing elsewhere prepared Luther to sing at Eisenach; and so closely is the town connected with his choral street-songs, that in thinking of it at this moment I seem to hear it echo with the voices of clustering youngsters on the steps of kind-hearted burghers at Christmastide, as they peep through an open door at the sparkling Christmas-tree, and accept the pfennige and groschen clapped in their tiny palms.

One afternoon, as I was rambling at the back of St. George's Church, a travelling companion, more zealous than myself, just then in search for Lutheran relics, said, with no small satisfaction, that she had discovered Luther's house. I must confess that at the moment a shade of scepticism crossed my mind, and I remarked, "Luther never could have had a house of his own at Eisenach, for he was, whilst living here, but a poor singing-boy."

FRAU URSULA COTTA SHOWS HOSPITALITY TO YOUNG LUTHER.
From the Painting of Prof. Lindenschmidt.

However, I soon saw how the matter stood ; and what was my delight upon actually finding the very threshold where Luther had poured his chorals into the ears of good Frau Ursula Cotta ! He and his merry party, as the story goes, sang at the doors of three houses in George Street without obtaining a single pfennig, and then reached the door-steps of Conrad Cotta, where, recognised as a boy whom Conrad's wife had noticed at church for his sweet voice and devout behaviour, he was invited indoors by the warm-hearted dame. She bestowed on him a gratuity, and soon began to treat him as a son, nourishing and comforting him by her snug fireside ; and so she unwittingly laid the foundation of her own world-wide fame,—for wherever the gospel of the Reformation is preached, that which this woman hath done shall be told for a memorial of her. She is to be classed with the widow of Sarepta and with the Shunammite wife ; and as I can never forget a lunch and siesta enjoyed years ago in a little garden linked to the name of the last-mentioned mother in Israel—a garden flashing with brilliant pomegranate blossoms, on the side of the Plain of Jezreel opposite to Carmel,—so neither shall I ever forget coming unexpectedly upon the house of Ursula Cotta in the town of Eisenach.

In reference to the schoolboy having been the guest of a benevolent lady, Dr. Waddington, in his " History of the Reformation on the Continent," ingeniously remarks that he " was in this respect more fortunate than the most formidable among the future adversaries of his doctrine, Ignatius Loyola, whom the same necessity compelled to persist for a much longer time, and at a much later period of life in the same practice." It is interesting to remember that, in after life, Luther seized the opportunity of repaying the kindness of his hostess, when Dame Ursula's son went to study at the University of Wittenberg, a circumstance skilfully interwoven into the " Chronicles of the Schönberg-Cotta Family."

The house at Eisenach now referred to bears Luther's name ;

part of it has been turned into a shop, where is sold a little pamphlet, containing a rude woodcut, with a curious history of the building. It appears to have been occupied by an order of German knights since Luther's time: memorials of which circumstance remain in rude bas-reliefs and Biblical inscriptions.

Two or three years ago Luther's name had not been placed over the door; I was told no relics of him were preserved within. But on my last visit I found it had become a show house, and a party of us were conducted up a dark old staircase on the left-hand side round the corner, to a room leading into another apartment, through a door of lattice-work. The woman who showed the house maintained that Luther slept in the inner room when a boy. In answer to inquiries as to the authority for such a statement, she averred that the Grand Duke supported it, and approved of the room being shown, which he would not do, she naïvely remarked, if the tradition were not correct. There is no resisting this.

In the printed account of the house Luther is connected with it through the hospitality of Frau Cotta; but in a guide-book to Eisenach and the Wartburg the house is more positively associated with the boy than with the lady, though how he could ever have lived there, except as her guest, is incomprehensible. We may then conclude that in some apartment of this rambling abode Luther dwelt; and from other traditions we may suppose that there he learned to play on the flute, and acquired that knowledge of music which, added to his original genius, made him a distinguished master of sacred melody.

Just by this house, at the back of St. George's Church, is a huge building, used as a brewery, said to have been originally the school-house in which Luther was taught as a boy, under the sway of Master Trebonius.

Nor is Eisenach associated with Luther's boyhood alone. Here he paused on his journey to Worms in the year 1521. He was taken ill before he left the town, and did not wholly recover

THE LUTHER HOUSE, EISENACH.

until he reached the city of Frankfort, whence he wrote to Spalatin on the 14th of April, saying how Satan had endeavoured to hinder him by more diseases than one; for, as he states, "all the way from Eisenach I was ill, and am still so, more than I ever was before."

Another and much more memorable visit to Eisenach was paid by Luther after his appearance at the Diet of Worms, and just before his residence in the Wartburg—each of which important incidents will be noticed hereafter. The visits to Eisenach now referred to occurred in the months of April and May, 1521; and it was upon the second visit, as he was returning from Worms, with a brighter halo of heroism round his brows than he had ever worn before, that his old friends besought him to preach. In compliance with their request, but in spite of a formal protest made by the parish priest, he ascended the pulpit of St. George's Church—the church where he had worshipped as a boy and attracted the notice of that kind-hearted parishioner, Frau Cotta—and addressed a crowded congregation, in which were many who, inclined to look amicably on the preacher and prepossessed in favour of the Reformation, were captivated by the force of his arguments and impressed by the pungency of his appeals. At the close of the sermon, the priest approached the Reformer, and begged pardon for having made a protest against his preaching, and avowed he had done so from fear of tyrants who were oppressing the Church.

Eisenach is still further associated with Luther through its being the residence of his staunch friend, Nicholas von Amsdorf, who zealously maintained the Reformer's views with such an amount of exaggeration, that he might be said to have been more Lutheran than Luther himself. Amsdorf lived in the Prediger Gasse, on the way to the Wartburg, No. 331. Here he died in the year 1565. His violence and indiscretion involved him in manifold difficulties, and he sought refuge with the young Duke of

Saxe-Weimar, calling himself *Exul Christi*—an exile for Christ. The elector, John Frederick, was his patron, and transferred him, after leaving Magdeburg, to the place of his final abode. He attended the elector in his dying hours, preached his funeral sermon, retained the friendship of his sons, and, amongst the later acts of his chequered life, superintended the Jena edition of Luther's works. He survived him nearly twenty years, having, by an interesting coincidence, been born in 1483—the date of the birth of his illustrious friend.

As the castle of the Wartburg, where Luther spent some of the most important months of his after life, crowns a charming hill to the south of the town, further associated memories of him meet us in this place. But we defer for the present the Wartburg portion of his story; though here we cannot help remembering that, as "Junker Georg," he would most likely steal into the streets of his dear Eisenach—"meine liebe Stadt," as he was wont to call it—and think of God's wonderful providence in leading "the blind by a way they knew not."

A later reminiscence of Eisenach must not be omitted.

"Rather more than half a century ago, in the year 1817" (says a daily journal), "a young Swiss student of theology set out from his native town of Geneva to enter himself at the University of Leipzig. He had no sooner crossed the German frontier than he found that a great movement was preparing among the people. On every side there was hurrying to and fro—enthusiasm, excitement, and suspense. At Frankfort the stranger ascertained, upon inquiry, that the forthcoming event was nothing less than the third centenary jubilee of the Reformation, about to take place in the great square of Eisenach, at the foot of the Wartburg Castle. In the town itself all the youths of the German universities were to meet some days before the actual celebration, in honour of the memory of Luther; and to Eisenach, accordingly, the Genevese student directed his steps. Night and day he travelled to arrive

EISENACH.

there in time, and at eight o'clock on the morning of the festival he was set down in the centre of the scene which his heart was bent upon witnessing. A crowd of students, dressed in costumes the most fantastic, filled the place. 'My designation,' wrote the young enthusiast many years later, 'as a Genevese student immediately opened to me the gate of that old castle in which the Reformation had been held captive in the person of its principal leader. But, alas! what called forth the enthusiasm of these young men was far less the faith of Luther than the reveries of demagogues. As for me, I beheld only the monk of Worms within the place of his captivity, and the idea of the Reformer took a powerful hold of my mind. I attended divine service in the church of Eisenach, and afterwards celebrated at Leipzig the festival of the jubilee itself. Wherever I went, memorials of the Reformation welcomed me, the bells rang out merrily, troops of students were singing, and the people were rejoicing. It was then I formed the design of writing the history of that great renovation.'"

The young Genevese was Merle d'Aubigné, who passed away to his rest, October 21, 1872; and the literary work which the spectacle at Eisenach suggested was the "History of the Reformation," in which the author has done so much to embalm with sweetest fragrance the name and deeds of Martin Luther.

IV.

Erfurt,

The Capital of Old Thuringia.

THE history of this place runs back to the days of Charlemagne. Being on one of the grand highways of Germany—that which connected Italy with the Baltic—it early became a scene of traffic and barter, and rose to the distinction of a town incorporated in the famous Hanseatic League Pirates by sea and robbers by land in unsettled times rendered some combination of interests among mercantile cities, along important lines of communication, essential to their safety and success; and Erfurt, protected and patronized by this primitive bond of commercial union, drove a thriving trade in the silks and the spices, the wools and the wares, which in waggons and on pack-horses passed through its ancient gates. Signs of its importance remain in its extensive and imposing fortifications; its numerous public buildings, seen from a distance, give the traveller an idea of former if not present prosperity; and its manufactures of various sorts continue to keep up some little amount of its mediæval reputation.

ERFURT, THE CAPITAL OF OLD THURINGIA.

It is many years ago since I first saw this interesting place; and I well remember the impression made by a ramble in its old-fashioned, quaint-looking streets. Differing from Eisenach in locality—for Eisenach stands at the foot of a fine mountain range adorned with woods, and Erfurt is built on a wide-spread plain, fruitful in hemp, flax, and oil seeds—it also differs from it in the general appearance of its thoroughfares; for whereas Eisenach is only near a small river, the Gera runs through the midst of Erfurt, and the stranger who crosses its little bridges will pause to glean amusement from curious vistas formed by overhanging houses, rickety landing-places, and dirty tan-yards on either side the running stream. The Dom, or cathedral, once belonging to a bishop, a highly ornamented building, combining beauty of detail with slenderness of construction, is the principal architectural lion, its portals, altars, and painted glass being well worth the archæologist's study; but I have a livelier recollection of the stately church of St. Severus, with its three spires, mounted on a hill, looking "like a direct lineal descendant from the old Roman basilican apse, grown into Grecian tallness."

There are two squares here—characteristic of German towns; the fish market, with a statue of Roland; the general market, with an obelisk in memory of the elector, Frederick Charles Joseph.

It is easy, putting aside whatever of modern architecture one meets with in Erfurt, to push back our thoughts to the sixteenth century, when the now dull town was bustling with wealthy merchants, and crowded with richly laden carts, and packed with temporarily lodged stores, and enlivened by troops of foreigners in varied national costume, and when it possessed another element of social life, now passed away; for Erfurt then contained a university with more than a thousand students, of which Luther said, "It was so celebrated a seat of learning that others were as grammar schools compared with it."

Hither came the miner's son, in the month of July, 1501, to

avail himself of the educational advantages which Erfurt offered; and here, from the age of eighteen to the age of twenty-two, the earnest youth might be seen sometimes with a sword at his side, according to the fashion of the day,—devouring Virgil and Cicero, digging into Aristotelian logic, engaging in debate with fellow-students, walking about the streets amongst the merchants and waresmen, or strolling out of the city gates into the pleasant neighbourhood of well-wooded hills, meadows, and streams. One spring day, as he took an excursion to the river Holme, through the golden mead, he ran the ungainly fashionable sword into his foot, which brought on consequences of a serious kind. In the prospect of death he commended himself to the Virgin, and used to say afterwards, "Had I then died, I should have died in the faith of the Virgin."

One incident in his Erfurt life stands out beyond the rest, and has been depicted by an eminent artist with singular force and beauty. You see Luther studying the Bible. It appears that he entered the University of Erfurt in 1501, when he was eighteen years old; and up to the age of twenty he had never seen an *entire* Bible. It must have been in the *university* library that he first laid hold of one. He was surprised to find in it so much more than he had ever read in the Gospels and Epistles prescribed for church use. He remarks, "I was reading a place in Samuel when it was time to go to lecture. I would fain have read the whole book through, but there was not opportunity then."

Two years afterwards he became a monk in the Augustinian monastery of the same town. "When I entered into the cloister," he narrates, "I called for a Bible, and the brethren gave me one. It was bound *in red morocco*. I made myself so familiar with it, that I knew on what page and in what place every passage stood." This is his own account—contained, according to Dr. Sears, in a MS. preserved in the library at Saxe-Gotha.[1] We have then his

[1] I have made unsuccessful attempts to verify this quotation; the librarian at Saxe-

LUTHER'S FIRST STUDY OF THE BIBLE.
From the Painting by E. M. Ward, R.A.

own authority for distinguishing between a copy of the Bible which he saw at the age of twenty in the *university* library, and a copy of the Bible which he procured in the *Augustinian monastery*, when he was twenty-two. The latter book was the one he studied, the "red morocco" cover ever after remaining in his memory; whilst, as we all are wont to do with regard to a familiar volume, he could, in imagination, turn over the pages and tell exactly where particular passages occurred. Luther's own account of this matter is more precise, detailed, and clear than that given by his friend and biographer, Mathesius. Mathesius describes it in the following manner: "Upon a time when Luther was carefully viewing the books one after another, to the end that he might know them that were good, he fell upon a Latin Bible, which he had never before seen in all his life. He marvelled greatly as he noted that more text, or more Epistles and Gospels, were therein contained than were set forth and explained in the common postils (or homilies) and sermons preached in the churches. In turning over the leaves of the Old Testament he fell upon the history of Samuel, and of his mother Hannah. This did he quickly read through with hearty delight and joy; and because this was all new to him he began to wish from the bottom of his heart that our faithful God would one day bestow upon him such a book for his own."

It is upon this passage in Mathesius, where the author describes in general terms Luther's first acquaintance with the Bible, and where he mixes up two incidents which occurred at different times, that Merle d'Aubigné founds his picturesque narrative.[1]

Unwarrantable inferences have been drawn from the world-

Gotha,—to whom my best thanks are due,—having in vain endeavoured to find the MS. But Dr. Sears must have seen the passage. He quotes it in his "Life of Luther," p. 66.

[1] "History of the Reformation." Religious Tract Society's Edit., p. 54. I may add that Köstlin as well as Sears distinguishes between Luther's reading the Bible in the university library and studying it in the university. See "Martin Luther," by Dr. Julius Köstlin, pp. 55, 65.

known incident now noticed. Some have concluded that scarcely any Bibles were at the time in print, whereas no less than ninety-one editions of the Vulgate are registered in Panzer between the years 1440 and 1500; even a German translation then existed, and was reprinted several times before the close of the fifteenth century.

Whilst these facts should be borne in mind, they cast no discredit upon Luther's statement, though they reflect upon certain conclusions reached by some modern writers. Copies of the Bible at that period, when reckoned together, appear numerous; yet after all they would form but a scanty supply for all Germany; and it is not at all inconsistent with what we know of the industry of German printers, to find that a lad, brought up on the edge of the Harz district, and at the foot of the Thuringian hills, should never have met with an entire copy of the Scriptures until he lighted upon one lying on the shelf of a university library.

Much of Luther's early religious history is bound up with the Thuringian capital. In a retired road which runs out of Erfurt to a place called Stotterheim, he was overtaken by a thunderstorm; the lightning struck at his feet and filled him with fear as he proceeded on his journey. Just before, he had lost a friend named Alexis, who, it seems, had been assassinated.[1]

Perhaps the electric shock blended its effects with his previous musings. At all events, stunned with terror at what he saw and felt, he uttered a prayer, and made a vow, common in those days, crying out, "Help, beloved St. Anne, and I will straightway become a monk!"

He fulfilled his promise. "I forsook," he says, "my parents and kindred, and betook myself, contrary to their will, to the cloister, and put on the cowl." One evening in July, 1505, he

---

[1] The supposition is, that he was killed by lightning at Luther's side, but this is a mistake.

ERFURT.

invited his university friends to a party in the house where he lived, and startled them at the close of the festivity by the solemn declaration, "To-day you see me: after this you will see me no more." He chose the convent of the Augustinian Eremites, and there spent the three following years of his life.

The convent was dissolved after the Reformation, and became converted into an orphan-house, called Martinsstift, in honour of the most illustrious inmate the building ever held. A fire broke out within the walls some time since, and consumed a considerable portion of the edifice, including a room most attractive to Luther pilgrims. At the time of my first visit the building was in its integrity—a quaint, rambling place, with queer old staircases and long wooden galleries, which blend with reminiscences of certain old London hostelries, such as the Tabard Inn in Southwark.

A dingy little room, after a lapse of years, reappears with a table and a chair which Luther was said to have used, the Reformer's portrait hanging on the wall, and the Bible he was reported to have studied occupying a place amongst the Protestant relics. People were apt fondly to imagine that the Bible there exhibited was that which young Martin found in the accidental way so often described; but this supposed what was impossible, and an inspection of the book sufficed to show the baselessness of the supposition. Around the cell, now destroyed, and the monastery, of which some parts remain, the history of the Reformer closely clusters, during that period when he was truly converted, and became a new creature in Christ Jesus.

Here it was that he began his novitiate, listening to the prior's words, "We receive you on probation for one year; and may God, who hath begun a work in you, carry it on unto perfection." After which the brotherhood said Amen, and chanted the "Magne Pater Augustine." Then came the changing a secular dress for the garments of the order, and the young man knelt down as antiphonies were sung and the benediction was invoked: "May God, who hath converted this young man from the world, and prepared for him a mansion in heaven, grant that his daily walk may be as becometh his calling, and that he may have cause to be thankful for this day's doings." A fraternal kiss all round in the convent hall finished the ceremony.

Here Luther took his vow in the second year. The bell was rung, the monks assembled, and the prior, standing before the altar steps, addressed him thus: "You have become acquainted with the severe life of our order, and must now decide whether you will return to the world." This was the reply: "I, brother Martin, do make profession, and promise obedience unto Almighty God, unto Mary, always a virgin, and unto thee, my brother, the prior of this cloister, to live in poverty and chastity after the rule of St. Augustine until death." A burning taper was put into his hand, prayer was offered by the brethren; and the initiated, when brought into the choir of the church, received once more the fraternal kisses. All was done sincerely and honestly by the young Saxon at the end of his novitiate. "When I was a monk," he wrote, " I was outwardly much holier than now. I kept the vow I had taken with the greatest zeal and diligence, by day and by night, and yet I found no rest, for all the consolations which I drew from my own righteousness and works were ineffectual." "Doubts all the while cleaved to my conscience, and I thought within myself, Who knoweth whether this is pleasing and acceptable to God or not?" "Even when I was the most devout, I went as a doubter to the altar, and as a doubter I came away again. If I had made my confession, I was still in doubt; if upon that I left off prayer, I was again in doubt; for we were wrapt in the conceit that we could not pray and should not be heard unless we were wholly pure and without sin, like the saints in heaven."

Here it was that Luther performed such menial offices as opening and shutting the convent gates, winding up the clock, sweeping the church, and cleaning the rooms; and out of these precincts he went into the streets of Erfurt, with a sack on his back, begging from house to house.

It is amusing to remember what he says in his "Table Talk" of the rivalry of different orders; how they ridiculed one another; how a barefooted friar compared a preaching brother, as it regarded his dress, to a swallow, black on the back and white on the breast; and how a preaching friar returned the compliment, by comparing, as to begging habits, the barefooted mendicant to a sparrow, which steals and devours.

Here it was that a brother burst into his cell one morning, because Luther had not opened his door at the usual time, and found him in a deep swoon. The music of the monk's flute restored the sufferer to consciousness and peace, as David's harp chased the evil spirit from Saul, the King of Israel.

Here it was—and this is most important—that Luther met with John von Staupitz, the Vicar-general of the Augustinians in Thuringia. Staupitz was far in advance of his age as regarded the knowledge of Christian truth; and in this new friend Luther found a spiritual helper of the highest worth. "In vain," said the young monk, "do I make promises to God; sin is ever the stronger of the two." "Oh, my friend," returned the more experienced officer of the community, "I have vowed more than a thousand times to the holy God to live piously, but never have I kept my vow. Now I have no wish to swear thus any more, for I know that I shall not keep it. If God refuse to be gracious to me for the love of Christ, and to give me a happy exit when called to leave this world, I could not, with all my vows and all my good works, stand before Him. I must perish." "Why will you torment yourself with high thoughts and speculations? Look to the wounds of Jesus Christ; to the blood which He hath shed for thee: it is there that thou wilt discover the grace of God. Instead of making thyself a martyr for thine offences, cast thyself into thy Redeemer's arms. Trust thyself to Him, to the righteousness of His life, to the expiation of His death."

Here it was that Luther entered upon the office of the priesthood. He relates with horror the utterance of the charge, "Receive power to offer sacrifice for the living and the dead;" he felt it a wonder, he vehemently said, that the earth did not open and swallow up both ordainer and ordained; and even at the time he faltered in the service, and was on the point of rushing from the altar in dismay. The idea of "standing before God without a mediator" struck him with terror, and some one by his side had to prevent his leaving the place. Yet he soon fell in with the accustomed mode of looking at the ceremony. "I was an unblushing Pharisee; when I had read mass and said my prayers I put my trust and rested therein. I did not behold the sinner that lay hidden under that cloak, not trusting in the righteousness of God, but in my own; not giving God thanks for the sacrament, but thinking He must be thankful and well pleased that I offered up His Son to Him; indeed, reproaching and blaspheming Him." So the matter appeared to Luther after he had abandoned Popery.

Here it was that further light dawned on his soul.

"When I began to meditate more diligently upon the words 'righteous' and 'righteousness of God,' which once made me fear when I heard them, and when I considered the passage in the second chapter of Habakkuk, 'The just shall live by his faith,' and began to learn that the righteousness which is acceptable to God is revealed without the deeds of the law—from that time how my feelings were changed! I said to myself, If we are made righteous by faith—if the righteousness which availeth before God saves all who believe therein,—then such declarations ought not to alarm a poor sinner and his timid conscience, but rather be a consolation." Again he remarks, "I had the greatest longing to understand rightly the Epistle of Paul to the Romans, but was always stopped by the word 'righteousness,' in the first chapter

LUTHER, BY ALBERT DURER.

and 17th verse, where Paul says, the righteousness of God is revealed in the gospel.

"My confused conscience cast me into fits of anger, and I sought day and night to make out Paul's meaning. At last I came to apprehend it thus: Through the gospel is revealed the righteousness which availeth with God; a righteousness by which God, in His mercy and compassion, justifieth us, as it is written, 'The just shall live by faith.' Straightway I felt as if I were born anew; it was as if I had found the door of paradise thrown wide open. Now I saw the Scriptures in an entirely new light, ran through their whole contents as far as memory would serve, and comparing them together found that the righteousness was surely that by which He makes us righteous, because everything agreed thereto so well. . . . The expression, 'The righteousness of God,' which I so much hated before, became dear and precious, my favourite and most comforting word; that passage of Paul was to me the true door of paradise."

Thus a memorable process in his experience began and ended with his Erfurt life. It commenced whilst he was taking a walk in the Stotterheim road; it reached its completion when he saw the Scriptures in a new light, and could rejoice in the righteousness which is of God by faith. The question has been often debated, When was it that John Wesley, in the course of his long spiritual conflict, might be said to be converted? And the same question might be raised in relation to the apostle Paul, had not artists, as well as divines, foreclosed it by giving the name of *conversion* to the event which occurred on the road to Damascus. From the Acts of the Apostles and the Epistle to the Galatians we learn that there were other initiatory stages in the history of Paul's spiritual life,—first, the three days' darkness in Damascus; and secondly, the three years' seclusion in Arabia. During that period the apostle was undergoing what he describes in the words, "It pleased God to reveal His Son in me." If his conversion was completed by those revelations of light and touches of grace which he received previously to his going up to Jerusalem, where his conversion was apostolically recognised,—it was only begun by that lightning-stroke of Divine power which arrested his steps before the gates of the Syrian capital. Paul's conversion covered a considerable space of time; so did Martin Luther's; so did Wesley's. We do not think that spiritual renewal can be brought under conditions of time and space, such as belong to physical events. It mysteriously proceeds to completion; and the date when the light breaks and the date when the sun shines forth may stand wide apart: throughout the truth and spirit of God are leading the soul along a path of experimental redemption—perhaps in certain moments leading the blind by a way they know not.

Erfurt is connected with Luther's history after his career as a Reformer had begun. In the year 1520 he left Wittenberg, then his home, to attend the Diet of Worms, and on his way touched at the town where he had been made monk and priest. Approaching the gates he was met by crowds of people shouting with joy, headed by the rector of the university, members of the senate, and distinguished burghers. Merle d'Aubigné imagines the Erfurt deputation turning their horses' heads after the meeting, and the cavalcade, with a concourse of pedestrians, accompanying the Reformer's carriage up to the city wall—the poor monk, who had often begged for the convent up and down the streets, being now welcomed in the great square with demonstrations of honour befitting the reception of a prince. He was received at the old convent, and there, according to a pathetic tradition, he saw a small wooden cross on the grave of a brother whom he had known, and who had died peacefully in the Lord. "See, my father," he said to Justus Jonas, "he reposes there, while I—" and then fixed his gaze on heaven. He returned shortly after to the same spot, and remained there until he was reminded that the monastery bell had tolled the hour for rest.

The Gospels for the day are, with some exceptions, the same in the Roman Catholic, the Anglican, and the Lutheran Church. The Gospel for the Sunday after Easter was then as it is now. Luther, therefore, took for his text John xx. 19, 20: "Then the same day at evening, being the first day of the week, when the doors were shut where the disciples were assembled for fear of the Jews, came Jesus and stood in the midst, and saith unto them, Peace be unto you. And when He had so said, He shewed unto them His hands and His side. Then were the disciples glad when they saw the Lord." The appropriateness of the passage to the circumstances at that moment is striking. Amidst the rage of controversy and the peril which threatened his liberty and his life, how full it was of comfort to Martin Luther to hear the Master's words of peace—how full of joy to see the Lord! Doubtless he felt all this, for he daily fed on the word of life. Yet his sermon that day ran on a different line. Preaching then was not so textual as it is now. A text was taken, but a preacher did not feel obliged to keep to it. It was a starting-point, from which he often wandered far and wide. Luther's mind was full of thought about the great business of his life—a reformation of the Church. So now he said, "There are two kinds of works —works extrinsic to us; those are good works—our own works, which are little worth. One man builds a church; another makes a pilgrimage to St. James's or St. Peter's; a third fasts, prays, puts on the hood, goes barefoot; another does something different still. All these works are nothing, and will perish; for our own works have no virtue in them. I am about to tell you what is the true work. God hath raised again a man—the Lord Jesus Christ—in order that He may crush death, destroy sin, and shut the gates of hell. Such is the work of salvation. The devil believed that he had the Lord in his power when he beheld Him between two thieves, suffering the most shameful martyrdom, accursed both of God and man. . . But the Divinity put forth its might, and annihilated death, sin, and hell. . . Christ hath won the victory! Here is the grand news!

and we are saved by *His* work, not by our works. The Pope says something very different. But I tell you the holy mother of God herself has been saved, not by her virginity, nor by her maternity, nor by her purity, nor by her works, but solely by means of faith, and by the works of God." This is a fair sample of his common strain of preaching. A crack in the wooden gallery whilst Luther was proceeding with his discourse alarmed the congregation, and they began to rush out. "Fear nothing," said he; "there is no danger; the devil would thus hinder the preaching of the gospel, but he will not succeed." And now the preacher touched on his text. "You speak much to us about faith; you will perhaps say to me, Teach us then how we may obtain it. Yes, indeed, I wish to teach you that. Our Lord Jesus Christ has said, 'Peace be unto you;' 'Behold My hands,' as much as if He had said, 'Behold, O man, it is I, it is I alone who have taken away thy sins, and who have redeemed thee; and now thou hast peace,' saith the Lord. Let us believe the gospel, let us believe St. Paul, not the briefs and decretals of the Popes." "Since God has saved us," he observed before he finished, "let us so order our works that He may take pleasure therein. Art thou rich? let thy goods be serviceable to the poor. Art thou poor? let thy services be of use to the rich. If thy labours be useless to all but thyself, the services thou pretendest to render to God are a mere lie."

"Not a word," remarks D'Aubigné, "about himself in Luther's sermon; not one allusion to the circumstances in which he stood; nothing about Worms, nor about Charles, nor about the nuncios: he preaches Christ, and Christ alone. At a crisis when the world had its eyes upon him, he is not in the least taken up about himself: and this is the mark of a true servant of God."[1]

---

[1] D'Aubigné's "History of the Reformation," p. 235.

V.

Rome, the Papal City.

AFTER Luther's removal from Erfurt to Wittenberg, in 1508, and his settlement there in the monastery of the Augustinians, and in connection with the university, he visited Italy on important business pertaining to his order. Disputes had arisen between the Wittenberg Augustinians and the Pope's vicar-general, and Luther travelled to Rome to secure a reconciliation.[1]

He travelled by way of Heidelberg, which he must have visited for some special purpose, as it was out of the direct route, and then proceeded through Suabia to Bavaria, and onwards to Milan, where he was received in "a marble convent," and found the brethren living sumptuously as in a palace.[2] At Pavia he was taken ill; at Bologna his illness appeared dangerous; and he particularly notices what caused his indisposition. "We slept at one time till six

---

[1] The date of the journey has been variously given, 1510, 1511, and 1512.

[2] "In Lombardy," he relates, "is a very rich Benedictine cloister, with a yearly income of 36,000 florins. Of eating and feasting there is no lack,—12,000 florins are consumed in the support of guests, and as large a sum is expended on the building. The residue goes to the brotherhood."

in the morning with our windows open, and when we awoke we found our heads so affected by catarrh, and so heavy and stupid, that we could travel that day only five miles." At Florence he was delighted with the hospital he visited.

What is called the Eternal City is not so much one city as a succession of cities. The city of the Republic, the city of the Emperors, the city of the Middle Ages, the city of the Renaissance period, and the city of the present day, are by no means the same, and one familiar with Rome just now would scarcely recognise the Rome of former ages.

Great changes were going on in the architecture of the place when Luther visited it, and greater changes followed.

Upon his reaching the Porta del Popolo he fell on his knees, raised his hands to heaven, and exclaimed, "Hail, holy Rome! made holy by the bodies of martyrs, and by the blood which has been spilt here!"—an exclamation sufficient to prove that, with his evangelical convictions, he retained a profound reverence for what he regarded as the mother city of Christendom.

He thus records his general impression: "Rome as it now appears is but a dead carcase compared with its ancient splendour. The houses rest on ground as high as the former roofs, so deep are the ruins of the old city. It is five miles in circumference. The vestiges of old Rome can scarcely be traced; but the Theatre and the Baths of Diocletian are still to be seen."

The reminiscences he preserved and recorded of his visit enable us to follow him in his rambles.[1]

"In the *Pantheon*, now converted into a church, are representations in painting of all the gods." "It has no windows, but one high vault, with an opening at the top to admit light. It possesses large marble columns scarcely compassable by two men with their arms extended."

---

[1] See "Luther," by Sears, pp. 112 *et seq.*

THE PANTHEON, ROME.

He visited the *Catacombs*. "By the Church of St. Calixtus (or St. Sebastian) there lie in one vault, as is said, more than 8,000 martyrs. Under the church, enclosed in sarcophagi, lie 176,000 holy bodies and forty-five martyred Popes."

ENTRANCE TO CATACOMBS.

"There is still to be seen in Rome a burial-place where there are, as is said, 80,000 martyrs and forty-six bishops." The catacombs were closed at the time Luther visited Rome— therefore he had not a solemn gratification, which I remember to have enjoyed, in common with thousands of other travellers, while exploring those mysterious recesses, where so many Christians have been buried, and where so many virgin tombs still wait for sleepers. Not from personal observation, but from current reports, did Luther derive what he relates, and therefore he may not himself be chargeable with the confusion and exaggeration of his statements.

The new *Cathedral of St. Peter* was at the time in process of erection, and he witnessed in it the exhibition of relics, including the famous Veronica—a handkerchief with which it is pretended the sweat was wiped from the face of the agonized Redeemer. "It is nothing but a black square board, with a cloth hung before it, and over that another, which is lifted up when the Veronica is shown. The poor besotted pilgrim can see nothing but a cloth before a black tablet." Thus he describes the relics years afterwards, when his eyes had been opened to Romish deceptions; but at the period of his visit he credulously gazed on such wonders, and felt more reverence than did most of his fellow-pilgrims.

Every one is familiar with the story of Luther crawling up Pilate's Staircase. The staircase is enclosed in a building near the Church of St. John Lateran, which, while possessing sumptuous additions made since the time that Luther was there, still retains some of its earlier interesting features,—the Byzantine cloisters, the ancient episcopal throne with a circular back, the mosaic of the apse, the wooden altar reserved for special occasions, the only one of the kind in Rome,—to mention no other objects. And then, as now, the traveller, standing under the portico of St. John, would be charmed with the view of the Sabine and Alban hills.

The staircase is said, in an absurd tradition, to have belonged to Pilate's palace in Jerusalem, and to be the same up which the Saviour ascended. It has attached to it two other staircases, by which pilgrims can descend after having mounted the sacred steps upon their knees.

When many years ago I saw a number of persons, some with an air of devotion, some with indifference or levity, crawling up the steps, I recalled to mind, as most Protestants do, the performance by Luther of this superstitious act, and the occurrence to his mind of the words of the apostle, "The just shall live by faith,"—a talisman for disenchanting the soul from all ritualistic delusions. I then thought, as many still do, that this passage flashed on him then for the first moment, and wrought a sudden change in his religious experience; but the fact is, as we have seen, that he had been previously struck with the apostle's words; he pondered them afterwards with increasing light; and his thoughts on the occasion of his visit were only links binding the experience of months and years into one chain of grace and salvation.

Luther did not leave Rome without being shocked at much which he saw. The Pope, he observes, moves as if making a triumphal entry, with richly caparisoned horses, and he bears the sacrament on a white palfrey. Luther witnessed masses irreverently performed, and what was more, saw worldliness, extravagance, pomp, vice, and crime abounding in the Holy City. "I myself," he declares, "have heard people say openly in the streets of Rome, 'If there be a hell, Rome is built upon it.'"

These recollections manifestly told on his after-life.

VI.

HEIDELBERG.

THERE is not a spot in Germany more familiar to English travellers than Heidelberg, nor one more remarkable for picturesque beauty. The river, the bridge, the castle, the town, the overhanging woods, the charming *Wolfsbrunnen*, the commanding *Königstuhl*, once seen, can never be forgotten, or thought of afterwards without a desire to revisit the charming spots.

The town and castle wear a certain air of antiquity; and yet only a small portion of either dates from an early period. In the five bombardments, the three pillages, and the two burnings it has endured, most of the old municipal and domestic buildings disappeared. Here and there a house, with a richly decorated front, remains to show what must have been the aspect of the town in days of yore. And though the castle is a pile of ruins, and all the red stones seem to have shared a common fate, an examination of the architecture, and the perusal of its history, evince how much of it was built within a compara-

HEIDELBERG.

tively modern period, and how small a portion can be traced back to the beginning of the sixteenth century. The well-known façade in the terrace, with statues of the reigning house of Bavaria, from Charlemagne and Otho of Wittelsbach, dates from 1607, in the time of Frederick IV; and the exquisite Rittersaal, of Italian architecture, was begun by Otho Henry, in 1556. The grim structure near the Portcullis Gate belongs to 1400; the gateway itself to 1355; and the oldest part of the castle was begun by the Elector Rudolph in 1300.

Histories and traditions of many kinds and ages gather round the halls and towers, especially the fates of Elizabeth and her husband, the King of Bohemia; but few persons think of Martin Luther while loitering about the old Court Yard. Yet his name comes into distinct connection with the place at a period when the buildings which now excite so much interest and admiration were not in existence, but the grand gateway, and Rudolph's fortress were prominent features, and the Castle must have had a thoroughly feudal look, speaking more of strength and defence than of beauty and ornament. The Chronicle of Heidelberg states that in 1510 Luther visited this city, when he was sent by the Convent of the Augustinians to the city of Rome. He was accompanied by Staupitz, but what was the exact object of the visit, and what happened to him whilst he was there, we do not know. Respecting a later visit, we have much information.

Writing on March 21, 1518, Luther tells his friend Lange, "I am besought by everybody not to go to Heidelberg, lest I be dispatched by fraud, if not by violence; but I shall fulfil my duty, and travel on foot." He passed this time by way of Judenbach, as will afterwards appear, and then stopped at Coburg. He speaks of the kindness of a parish priest to him at Weissenfels, and on the 19th of April says, "We arrived at Würzburg on the 17th, and presented our letters to the illustrious Bishop. He desired to send an attendant with me all the way to Heildelberg. But only one thing did I ask of him, and that was a safe-conduct, which I have received." This is remarkable, as the journey occurred after the publication of the Wittenberg theses.

Of certain theses, which he propounded at Heidelberg, twenty-eight related to theology, and twelve to philosophy; free will, grace, original sin, predestination, are affirmed, and justification by faith is asserted in the following terms: "He is not justified who does many works, but he who without works has much faith in Christ. The Law says, 'Do this,' and it is never done. Grace says, Believe in Him,' and all things are straightway performed."

We have two accounts of the Heidelberg Conference. One by a young man, a native of Alsace, at the time a student in the University of Heidelberg. He was twenty-eight years old, full of promise and hope, a scholar and a theologian, destined to take a conspicuous part in the Church's reformation. It was no other than Martin Bucer, who, according to a fashion in that age, had translated his German name into Greek, Kuhhorn, or Cow's horn, became Bucer; as Gerard became Erasmus; Hauschein, or House light, Œcolampadius; and Schwarzerde, or Black earth, Melancthon.

Bucer gives an account of the visitor to Heidelberg in the following words: "A theologian, though not of our university, has just been here, who treats with utter contempt all our Sophistical and Aristotelian trifling, and addicts himself wholly to the Scripture. It was Martin [Luther], the famous flouter of indulgences, who has here maintained, after the accustomed fashion, those paradoxes which not only astonished all who heard them, but to most seemed even heretical." "Remarkable both for the mildness of his replies and the patience of his attention, he exhibited in the solution of difficulties the acumen of Paul rather than of Scotus, so concise were his answers, so much to the point, so readily borrowed from the storehouse of the sacred oracles. He was the admiration of all. On the day following I had a familiar and friendly conversation with him at a supper, not adorned by dishes, but by doctrines; and he explained to me with perspicuity everything that I asked him. He agrees in all respects with Erasmus, but surpasses him in this, that what the latter insinuates only, he openly and freely teaches."[1]

Luther, writing to Spalatin, May 18, 1518, relates, "The illustrious Prince Wolfgang, Count Palatine, and Master James Simler, and Hase, Master of the Palace, received me with much honour. The Count invited us—that is, Father Vicar Staupitz and our Lange, now Provincial Vicar; we had pleasant conversation together, and greatly enjoyed ourselves, eating and drinking, seeing the decorations of the palatinate fortress, the armoury, and other objects in this truly regal castle. Master James could not enough praise the letter of our Prince, saying, in the Neckar dialect, 'You have, by God, splendid credentials.' Indeed nothing was wanting which could be desired.

"The doctors freely allowed me to dispute, and differed so modestly as to commend themselves by these means. And although my theology appeared to them strange, they argued in opposition fairly and pleasantly, except one, the fifth in order, a young man who moved the audience to laughter, by saying, 'If the country people heard you they would stone you to death.' My theology was a bitter pill to the Erfurt divines, especially to one [Dr. Jodocus] of Eisenach. I had a discussion, and at least made him understand that he could neither prove his own propositions nor confute mine.

"With Doctor Usingen I rode out in a carriage, and endeavoured to convince him. I do not know whether I succeeded, but I left him full of thought and wonder. The fact is, these men are inveterate in their mistaken opinion. It is otherwise with the

---

[1] *Martin Buceri ad B. Rhenanum Relatio Historica, &c.* Waddington's "History of the Reformation," i. 119.

young; they are open to conviction, and my hope is that as Christ, rejected by the Jews, turned to the Gentiles, so now His own true Theology, which the old oppose, will transfer itself to the young."

The account Luther gives of his visit does not distinctly say that he lodged in the castle; his language may simply mean that he went up to see the Prince for a brief entertainment, his residence for a time being elsewhere. As he went to the town on

LUTHER'S HOUSE, NEUENHEIM.

business of his order, that would be transacted at some Augustinian convent; and we might presume that there he would lodge.

We read in Murray's Hand-book, that "at the village of Neuenheim, which is on the right bank of the Neckar, nearly opposite to the railway station, in a house that goes by the name of Mönchhof, according to an obscure tradition, Luther was lodged, when he passed through Heidelberg in 1518." His only visit to the place that year was the visit just described; and it is possible that here some confused recollection appears of his being lodged outside the town, during the progress of the business which he had come to transact. Many years ago, on a summer evening, I drove over to see the house, but noticed nothing remarkable in its appearance. I must refer again to Heidelberg in the next chapter.

VII.

BASLE.

IN 1879 an interesting Conference was held in Basle, when members of the Evangelical Alliance from different parts of the world —in connection with a survey of the present state of Protestant Christendom, and the duties arising out of it,—celebrated the Reformation which occurred in that city above three centuries and a half before. Though Basle is now decidedly Swiss, it was at that period more decidedly German, and was brought into manifold relations, of a Protestant kind, with other parts of Europe—even with England, as well as Saxony. English Reformers found refuge there in the days of Queen Mary, and in 1529, when Œcolampadius was in the ascendant, and "reiterated cheers," as Merle d'Aubigné says, "greeted the work of the Reformation," of course the eyes of the citizens would be turned towards the brave Monk of Wittenberg, who fought his battle with Rome after a different fashion from theirs, and who, on the subject of the Eucharist, entertained views contrary to those of the Swiss Divines. The very year just mentioned, 1529, saw Œcolampadius and Zwingle at Marburg, on the Lahn, in stout controversy with the advocate of consubstantiation; he, as I shall shew,[1] insisting on the literal signification of the words, " This is My body "; they, especially Zwingle, contending it was impossible that a material body could exist in different places at the same moment. The relations between Luther and the Swiss were by no means amicable, and it is sad to hear him saying to the latter, in the Castle of Philip the Magnanimous " You have a different spirit from ours ; our conscience opposes our receiving you as brethren." Nevertheless, the Swiss were ready to do justice to the character and work of the great champion of German Reform ; and his name was on the lips and hearts of many of their descendants who crowded the Hall of the Vereinshaus, and the aisles of St. Martin's Church.

One day, as I was walking up a narrow street of the quaint old city, a friend asked me, " Have you been to see Luther's house ? " The question startled me, as I did not remember having noticed, in the numerous memoirs of Luther, any reference to his having ever visited Basle. Though not receiving evidence of Luther's presence in the place, I could not deny the possibility of his coming at one time or other within the walls ; and, therefore, accepted an invitation to go and look at what was mentioned under the name of Luther's house. It stands, if I remember right, not far from the Basle Museum, and is now employed as a bookseller's shop. Indeed, Protestant publications are there supplied; and it is regarded by some as a sort of centre for Evangelical literature ; an association highly becoming the name which the small old unpretentious building is now made to bear. I presume there must be some local tradition upon which the idea rests ; but whether trustworthy or otherwise I could not ascertain. Supposing that there is authority for the belief I heard expressed, it remains an important question, When did Luther visit Basle ? It appears to me extremely improbable he could have been there after the Marburg Conference, or even any short time before, when the

[1] Page 187.

momentous controversy as to the Eucharist was agitating so violently the minds of German and Swiss Reformers. Had Luther appeared then amongst the brethren round the red sandstone cathedral which there crowns the Rhine, it must have created an excitement not to be forgotten, and would have been sure to find a conspicuous place in history. If Luther went to Basle at all, it must have been before he became widely known; indeed, before the Diet of Worms, and before the nailing of his theses on the Wittenberg Church-door. He was at Heidelberg in 1518,[1] and tradition, as we have noticed, points to a house he lodged in at Neuenheim, on the right bank of the Neckar. But it is very unlikely he then proceeded so far as Switzerland, since he makes no mention of such a journey in his correspondence. Hence we are driven back to earlier Wittenberg days, when he was working hard in his professorship; and there, in 1510, we find him as already described, starting for Rome, as a deputation from his Augustinian convent. We are expressly told he then took Heidelberg in his way, certainly a roundabout route for reaching the papal city. Then we learn he went through Suabia into Bavaria. A near road in that direction would be far enough away from Basle; yet as circuitous routes then were not uncommon, and as there might be convent business to transact at Basle as well as Heidelberg, it is not *impossible* that, before he was known to history, he might have paid a passing visit, of which a remembrance lingers only in the local tradition I have noticed.

Before leaving Heidelberg altogether, I may be permitted to say that in the University library, looking at volumes of different kinds, I felt special interest in examining some early Bibles. It is a common and a great mistake to suppose that Luther was the first person to translate the Scriptures into German; and also to suppose that he had never seen a Bible until he found a copy in the Dominican convent. He tells a different story himself, as I

[1] See p. 71.

have pointed out in my fourth chapter. A distinction must be made between the Bible in the University Library, which surprised him so much when he glanced at it, and the red morocco volume in the monastery with which he made himself so familiar two years afterwards. Ninety-one editions of the Vulgate are, as I have said, registered in Panzer between the years 1440 and 1500; therefore, Luther's ignorance, when he was twenty, only shows that the book was little known in the University and the Convent of Erfurt; not that it had not been often printed in Germany during the previous half century. It seems wonderful that a young monk should never have heard of the vernacular version then in existence; at any rate, the knowledge of the Word of God, as a whole, must have been exceedingly rare in the old Thuringian capital. Let us not, however, overlook the fact that the brethren knew where to find the "red morocco" copy, when Luther called for a Bible.

The discovery of early-printed Latin Bibles has advanced since Panzer's time, and it must be interesting to an English reader to know that at the Caxton Exhibition of 1877 there were shown above fifty distinct editions printed between that of Mentz, by Gutenberg, about 1450 and 1455, and that of Venice, by Paganini, 1501, four years before Luther entered on his novitiate. "Some half-dozen huge folio Bibles in Latin and German, beside the magnificent Psalters of 1457 and 1459, had appeared in type before a single volume of the classics saw the 'new lamp of the new learning.' All the earliest printed Bibles were in the Latin vulgate, the first complete edition of the Septuagint not having been issued from the press of Aldus till the year 1518, and by that time no less than fourteen German Bibles had issued from the press. Twelve grand patriarchal editions of several different translations appeared before the discovery of America."[1] The first German Bible is attributed to the year 1466. A copy of it, printed at Strasburg, and beautifully illuminated in gold and

[1] Catalogue of the Loan Collection exhibited at Kensington, 1877.

colours, was lent to the Kensington Exhibition by Her Majesty the Queen. A twelfth German edition, in two volumes, with woodcuts, dated 1490, was also exhibited.

I can never forget the delight with which, for the first time, I turned over the pages of an illustrated German Bible at Heidelberg. Grotesque woodcuts were sprinkled about from end to end. The formation of Eve out of the side of Adam, Noah's Ark sailing on the waters, with a multitude of other subjects, figured to one's great amusement on the crisped leaves. Facts of this kind, and they might be multiplied, are sufficient to dispel common misconceptions which have gathered round the anecdote of Luther studying the Bible in the Erfurt monastery.

VIII.

THE FREE CITY OF AUGSBURG IN 1518 AND 1530.

FEW German cities are to English travellers better known than Augsburg. Many a tourist on his way to Italy, or on diverging from the beaten path to Switzerland, here "turns aside to tarry for a night." And a very pleasant place it is, in which to while away a few holiday hours. The Maximilian Strasse is a noble thoroughfare, long, and for a considerable distance very wide, lined with old houses quaintly gabled, jutting out into richly decorated oriel windows, or painted over with huge frescoes, representing Scripture facts or ecclesiastical legends. The Rathhaus is an Italian structure of palatial style and grandeur, recalling days still more prosperous than the present in commercial traffic and monetary exchanges. The Tower of Perlach, with its five hundred steps, is a belfry of the Renaissance type, near the Rathhaus, and raises anybody who likes to perform the arduous task of climbing it, to the summit of that building. The hotel of the "Three Moors," where most tourists stop, was once the mansion of Anthony Fugger, the famous Augsburg merchant who entertained Charles V. In a cedar-ceiled apartment—carrying one back to the sixteenth century—the generous money-lender burnt the royal bond, and made his guest a present of the loan. By a winding stone stair leading from the room you can go and explore mysterious nooks and corners, the whole house retaining still a pungent flavour of antiquity. The three bronze fountains in the

AUGSBURG.

main highway—one close to the "Three Moors"—are curious works of art, repaying longer examination than is generally spent on them. The cathedral and other churches, by no means superior, are sure to be visited; and a portal, a window, and a piece of sculpture here and there excite some interest. In the lower part of the city there are odd-looking places, which gratify those who are in search of the picturesque and the archæological; and it is agreeable to repeat in imagination a stroll I once had by the side of little water streams running on the edge of gardens and at the foot of summerhouses; all cheerful to look at on a fine summer's day, and stimulating minds of the Izaak Walton cast to musings fit for Sundays as well as working days. Our interest in Augsburg just now belongs mainly to one spot, which we are enabled to identify.

Luther reached Augsburg on an autumn evening in the year 1518, just after a grand Diet of the empire had been held. He had been summoned to meet Cardinal Cajetan, a man devoted to the service of Rome, and just then much concerned at what he heard of the course pursued by the young Reformer; for by this time Luther had become well known in that character. The spiritual change wrought in him at Erfurt had brought him more closely to examine the principles and practices of the Romish communion. The wretched sale of indulgences by Tetzel had aroused his indignation, and filled him with honest longings for ecclesiastical reform. At Wittenberg the development of this passion had been going on; and already he had affixed to the door of a church in the city his theses upon indulgences.

No wonder ecclesiastical authorities began to call him to order. So, in obedience to a command from Cardinal Cajetan, authorized to examine and try the troublesome priest, Luther left Wittenberg on foot, and reached Weimar on the 28th of September, when he preached in the palace church; and tramping on to the place of his destination, he was so exhausted and threadbare at last, that a few miles from the gates of Augsburg he obtained a carriage and borrowed a gown from a Nuremberg friend, in order to make a better appearance before his ecclesiastical superior. Upon his arrival in the city he went to lodge at the monastery of the Augustinians, the order to which he belonged.

On the 11th of October Luther thus addressed Melancthon, with whom he had already become intimate: "There is nothing new or strange here, saving that the whole city is filled with the rumour of my name, and everybody is eager to see the new Erostratus who has kindled such a conflagration. . . . I will sooner perish, and, what is most grievous, for ever lose your delightful converse, than recall what has been rightly said, and become the occasion of extinguishing good learning. Italy is covered with Egyptian darkness, together with those sottish and savage enemies of letters and of study. They neither know Christ nor the things of Christ, and yet they are our lords and masters in matters of faith and of morals."

Other letters written from Augsburg are full of lifelike touches. We can see him in the Maximilian Strasse—as he is now approaching middle age—with a face which has lost a little of its plumpness, and eyes which retain their early fire, and wearing the gown lent him by his Nuremberg friend; the people gape after him as he marches with a step that shows he can stand and walk alone, even in the presence of cardinals and kings.

Cardinal Cajetan lodged in a building repeatedly called in the story of this Augsburg trial "the palace." The palace, or *schloss*, still remains, close to the cathedral. There the Bishops in former days resided; and where but there could a Cardinal, travelling in pomp, and for an important ecclesiastical purpose, put up on a visit to the grand old city? The palace is now a good deal altered, and promises little, from its external appearance, to gratify searches after localities connected with circumstances which occurred above three hundred years ago. It was not until a third visit to Augsburg that I thought of exploring this edifice; and then I did so in consequence of the suggestion of a persevering friend, who had been repaid for enterprising curiosity by a sight of the interior. I had some trouble in ascending out-of-the-way staircases, and wandering through far-reaching corridors, before anybody could be found to answer a question, when I lighted upon an intelligent gentleman, who conducted me to the north-west corner of the building near a tower, and pointed out state apartments connected with Charles V.'s visit, to be noticed presently.

Most likely in the same part of the building, the representative of the papal court, a Cardinal Prince of Rome, would be accommodated and entertained. The rooms are modernized now; one has gilded ceiling and walls, with portraits of Emperors in the panels. A grand staircase leads up to it, and it is easy to imagine the sort of appearance the place presented in 1518. Here, then, we may localize the story of Luther's interviews with Cajetan.

"Come," said a fussy official, "the Cardinal is waiting for you. I am going myself to take you to him. You must be taught how to comport yourself in his presence. On entering the hall where you are to find him, you must throw yourself prostrate, with your face on the ground. When he has told you to rise you will place yourself on your knees, and you must wait till he bids you, before you stand upright."

These directions were given in the monastery of the Augustinians, the site of which I have not been able to identify; but Augsburg had other monasteries—one belonging to the Carmelites, under a prior named John Frosch, who invited his black-frocked friend to come and tarry with the white-gowned brethren.

The chapel of the Carmelite convent now bears the name of St. Anna's Church, and is situated in the Anna Strasse. It is of Gothic architecture, and has an altar at each end. That at the west has an organ close to it, with two wings attached, said to be painted by Holbein the younger, a native of the town. At the same end, on the south side, is the burial-place of the Fugger family, containing a tomb in the form of the Church of the Holy Sepulchre at Jerusalem. The church contains portraits of Luther and Frederick the Wise. The former is attributed to Cranach.

In the room connected with Charles V. at the "Three Moors"

there hangs an old map of Augsburg, dated 1626. It exhibits the old walls, gates, streets, and public edifices; and on it I discovered he church of St. Anna, with monastic buildings and garden attached. With this map in my mind, I questioned the old woman who played the part of cicerone, and who was a great oddity, bu very good-tempered. My friends and myself had a good deal of difficulty to make her understand the points of the compass, and to give an idea of the bearings of the church; and parrot-like, as most of her race are found to be, she pertinaciously adhered to her own routine of explanation, and seemed greatly discomfited at any cross-questioning, with a view of obtaining information on points out of her usual line. However, when we passed from the church into the remains of the monastic buildings, she seemed to brighten up and to warm at the mention of Luther.

Having shown us a sepulchral chapel to the memory of the Oesterreicher family, she took us into the cloisters, which are in excellent preservation, and contain numerous mural monuments, sepulchral slabs, and finely embossed brasses. Then pointing to a little window over the cloister wall, looking down into the enclosed garden, she told us that was the room where Luther lodged when at Augsburg. Thus tradition and the map concurred to satisfy us that we were veritably on the Reformer's track; and there remained no reason for doubting that Luther had paced these very cloisters, and worshipped within this very church.

In the course of Luther's interviews with Cajetan, the Reformer had the benefit of advice and intercession tendered by Staupitz, the Vicar-general of the Augustinians, who retained a strong personal affection for his friend of former years. Staupitz was asked by Cajetan to try and persuade Luther to recant. Staupitz told Cajetan that the attempt would be useless, for Luther was too strong for him in Scripture arguments. However, he did try; but when Martin returned to his Bible defences, Staupitz found himself without any means of hopeful attack, and at last encouraged rather than accused his friend; for, said he, "remember, dear brother, that thou hast taken this matter up in the name of Jesus."

Accompanied by the Carmelite prior, Dr. Link, and an Augustinian monk, Luther proceeded to the palace, and was there received by the Cardinal in the accustomed form. Surrounded by his Italian attendants, in a room such as I have indicated, or in one near it, Cajetan said to Luther there were two propositions which he had advanced, that he ought to retract. First, that the treasure of indulgences is not composed of the merits and sufferings of our Lord Christ; and secondly, that faith is essential to the efficacy of the holy sacrament.

Such retraction was the end sought in repeated conversations; such retraction Luther would not make, but declared in one of the interviews—and it is the pith of all his utterances at Augsburg—"that no man can be justified before God unless by faith; so that man must believe with an entire assurance that he has obtained grace. To doubt this grace is to reject it. The faith of the righteous man is his righteousness and his life." His soul, Luther avowed, sought only for truth; nor was he so proud and so covetous of vain-glory as to be ashamed of retracting what he knew to be false. It would be his joy to see the triumph of God's truth, only he would not do anything contrary to the voice of his conscience.

Of course, all the talk at Augsburg between the nuncio and the monk proved in vain, and it cannot be better summed up than in the words of the latter: "The legate hath treated with me, or rather against me, now for the space of four days, having finely promised our illustrious Prince that he would act a kind and fatherly part, but, in truth, doing everything by inflexible power alone. He was loth to have me debate the matters in dispute with him publicly; nor was he willing to discuss them with me privately. His replies were all of this one tenor,—'Recant; acknowledge your error; the Pope will have it so, and not otherwise, whether you will or not.' . . . At length, overcome by the entreaties of many, he consented that I should give my reasons in writing, which I have done this day in the presence of the Elector's minister, Felitzsch. The paper was rejected with disdain, and my revocation loudly demanded. : . . I essayed a dozen times to say a word, and he chopped in upon me as many times with thundering tones. . . . As he cried ' Recant!' I left him; when he added, ' Go! and return not to me till thou art willing to recant.' "

Luther, after his final audience, wrote the Cardinal a letter, in which he apologized for rude expressions he had used relative to the reigning pontiff, and professed himself ready to apologize for them from the pulpit. Moreover he promised not to say a word as to the matter of the indulgences, if this affair could be arranged. He concluded by praying, with all humility, that the whole business might be referred to "our most holy lord the Pope," that the Church might decide the question, so that he himself might honestly retract or sincerely believe.

This letter has been used to his disadvantage. He has been charged with tergiversation, hypocrisy, and the like. Merle d'Aubigné, his Dutch annotator, and others, have warmly defended him, praising him for frankness in acknowledging that he spoke unadvisedly with his lips.[1] But Luther's words in his letter go beyond a gentleman's apology for unguarded language. He left the whole matter, which up to that hour, he says, had been doubtful, "to our most holy lord Leo X., in order that the Church may decide, pronounce, and ordain, so that one may retract with a good conscience or believe with sincerity." This was inconsistent with Luther's habitual appeals to Scripture, and with the whole drift of his conversation with Cajetan. Is it not wiser and more just, to admit that Luther was an impetuous man, and

---

[1] D'Aubigné's "History of the Reformation." See the whole of book iv., on Luther before the legate, also Sears, 202 *et seq.*

experienced changeful currents of feelings; that at times he was disposed, if possible, to heal the breach with Rome; and that now, without any consciousness of doing what was deceptive, or of saying what was untrue, he used language which went a great deal further than he himself was prepared to go? Good men are often inconsistent, and it is no use attempting to gloss over inconsistencies when they plainly appear. The same line of remark is applicable to the very submissive letter which Luther wrote to the Pope the 5th of March, 1519.

Luther reached Augsburg on the 7th of October; by the 19th it was time for him to be off. His friends saw as plainly as himself that the Italians were not to be trusted. The fate of John Huss diminished the value of imperial safe-conducts, and therefore that which Luther had in his pocket by no means insured him against the prison and the stake. So, on Wednesday morning, the 20th, he rose before daybreak, and by stealth set off on his journey. He mounted a pony left for him by Staupitz, and started without bridle, boots, spurs, or any weapon of defence, under the guidance of a trusty officer, through a wicket gate in the city wall opened for him by order of a friendly magistrate.

Some old walls remain, and conspicuously a gate called the Frauen Thor, with its portcullis, the upper part of the building being of the sixteenth or seventeenth century; but I discovered nothing in the direction of Nuremberg, or in any other direction, which could afford an idea of what the fortifications were in the time of Luther. On the old map the fortifications are distinctly portrayed, from which it appears they were elaborate and curious, with a broad ditch surrounding the city, and crossed by drawbridges. Over one of these, probably, Luther crept to mount the pony furnished by his friend, after which he would scour the road to Nuremberg by Donauwörth and Nördlingen, before the place attained historic fame, no Marlborough then having ploughed the fields with artillery, and sown the furrows with balls and bullets.

"Our soul is escaped as a bird out of the snare of the fowler: the snare is broken, and we are escaped. Our help is in the name of the Lord, who made heaven and earth." Thus Luther sung in his heart as he rode along from Augsburg to Nuremberg; and when he reached his home, on the 31st of October, he wrote to Spalatin, telling him, "To-day have I come, by the grace of God, safely to Wittenberg, not knowing, however, how I shall abide here, for I am in a state of uncertainty between hope and fear. Yet," he adds, "I am full of joy and peace, so much so as to marvel that this my trial should appear a great matter to many notable men."

Twelve years afterwards another extraordinary scene connected with the Reformation occurred at Augsburg, when, as D'Aubigné says, "Luther was present, though invisible." In the summer of 1530 a Diet was held. The Emperor Charles V., then thirty years of age, travelled from Innsbruck to Munich, and onwards to Augsburg, to meet there the representatives of the empire. On the 15th of June the gate of the city on the Munich side witnessed a splendid procession. There were the Electors and their households, with gorgeously apparelled followers in splendid uniforms. Over bright cuirasses and scarlet doublets floated many-coloured plumes. Some of the horsemen's liveries were liver-coloured, some grey, some red. Pages were clad in yellow and crimson; robes were of velvet and of silk. Heralds, trumpeters, drummers, and grooms swelled the moving throng. The Elector of Saxony, a friend of Luther, and a champion of the Reformation, carried the imperial sword before Charles, whose garments glittered with precious stones, as, crowned with a little Spanish hat, he rode on a white horse, under a canopy of red, white, and green damask, borne by six senators of Augsburg. The cavalcade passed through the gate between the hours of eight and nine of a long summer's day, met by the Burgomaster and Councillors of the city, and saluted by rounds of artillery from the ramparts, by peals from the church bells, and by the blast of trumpets, the rattling of drums, and the shouts of the people. The Emperor immediately proceeded to the Cathedral, where he fell on his knees before the altar, and was afterwards conducted to his lodgings in the palace. There he was entertained in regal splendour, and there was presented to him the famous Augsburg Confession.

We were told that in the large room at the corner of the quadrangle near the tower, at the west corner, the presentation of the Confession took place. The room was much larger than it is now; and a conductor on one of my visits intimated that it had formed part of a chapel. At all events, according to the records of the transaction, it was in the chapel of the Augsburg palace that the memorable transaction occurred. The chapel could not hold more than two hundred people; but before three o'clock, the time appointed for the ceremony, the quadrangle was crowded by multitudes hoping to see or hear something of what went on. Charles sat in a chair of state, with the great men of the empire on either side; and when he commanded a Latin copy of the Confession to be read, John, the Elector of Saxony, uttered the words so often quoted, "We are Germans, on German soil, and I hope your majesty will allow us to speak in our own tongue." Bayer, one of the Chancellors of the Elector, then read the document in a tone so loud and clear, that it was heard outside by those who stood in the court near the open windows.

The Confession includes articles respecting the Holy Trinity, the fall of man, human depravity, and the incarnation of Christ, couched in orthodox phraseology. Indeed, it is expressly stated that the Protestant did not differ from the Catholic Church in articles of faith: and, though the Protestant doctrine of justification is insisted upon in the fullest manner, Melancthon, who drew up the Confession, and those who united in presenting it, did not regard that doctrine as contrary to the faith of the Catholic Church taught by the Fathers; and it is a well-known fact that there were at the crisis of the Reformation in the Roman Catholic communion, men such as Contarini, who approached in theological opinion on this subject very near to Martin Luther. Any Antinomian perversion of the doctrines of grace was carefully guarded against in the Augsburg manifesto; and it is declared that the Protestants were deserving of praise for showing the only effectual way in which holiness could be attained, namely, through faith in Christ.

A surprising tone of moderation in reference to some points in dispute characterises this document. The administration of the sacrament in both kinds, the marriage of priests, and the abolition of masses for the sins of the living and the dead, are demanded; and the worship of saints, "a distinction of meats and other traditions," monastic vows, and the power of pontiffs over secular princes, are condemned; but, in terms rather equivocal, it is affirmed that the practice of confession was not abolished by the reformed, only the people were instructed that an enumeration of their offences was unnecessary, and, indeed, impossible. No protest is made against the spiritual power of the Pope; and the whole composition manifests that caution and that unwillingness to give offence which formed so marked a feature in the character of Philip Melancthon.

Into the history of the results of this Confession it is foreign to enter. All which needs to be said is, that the Emperor, when he had heard the paper read, requested the Protestant princes not to make it public.

Luther was not present; but he came as near to the scene of action as he could, tarrying the whole summer at Coburg, on the edge of the dominions under Protestant rule. "How I wish," he said to Melancthon, "I could be allowed to come to you! I burn with desire to come, unbidden and uninvited." How he spent his time at Coburg will soon appear.

LEIPZIG TOWN HALL (RATHHAUS).

IX.

LEIPZIG IN THE YEAR 1519.

THERE is not much in Leipzig to interest the traveller, unless he happens to enter it during fair-time. Then, according to all accounts, the temporary booths erected in the streets and squares recall the Feast of Tabernacles at Jerusalem; and the costumes of sojourners, and the languages in which they speak, are as varied as they could have been on the day of Pentecost. But a different purpose from that which brought people to the metropolis of Palestine gathers together larger multitudes three times a year at Leipzig, for they come, in some instances for pleasure, but in greater numbers for merchandize; these fairs are marts for all sorts of wares, especially books. This old German town forms an emporium of printers and booksellers, as is testified by the existence of the Deutsche Buchhändler Börse, a place of exchange established for the use of the sons of Minerva.

At common times the most agreeable part of Leipzig is found in the public gardens round the walls, studded plentifully with hotels and cafés. Penetrating the interior of the city, I have more than once plunged into a network of gloomy streets, with tall unpicturesque buildings on either side, and, hoping to find something more attractive, have at length by chance stumbled unexpectedly on the great market-place, where the houses are so numerous that they are crushed out of due dimensions by being closely packed together; the Rathhaus standing amongst them, with considerable pretensions to magnitude and dignity. The Königshaus is not without architectural interest; but the chief lion, after all, is Auerbach's cellar—a vault under the house next door to the Königshaus, where, according to a famous tradition, Dr. Faustus performed his feats, still represented in rude daubs remaining on the walls. Goethe has chosen the place for a scene in his tragedy of "Faust;" here it is that he makes the students of the Leipzig University drink wines mysteriously supplied out of the gimlet-holes in the table, through the incantations of Mephistopheles. Goethe's shadow falls on most visitors as they descend the steps to this drinking-room; but there is another and a nobler which haunts the place; for, in the house occupied by the man who gives his name to the cellar, Martin Luther was entertained when engaged in the memorable Leipzig disputation. "Those who were friendly to us," remarks the Reformer, "came to us privately, but Auerbach, a man of excellent genius, and the younger Pistoris, invited me to their houses." Dr. Sears, in his sketch of the spiritual history of Luther, notices how interesting it is to find "that Luther was a guest with that very Auerbach whose cellar has become so celebrated in connection with the name of Dr. Faust;" and this identification of a well-known resort in Leipzig market-place, with the hospitalities of Auerbach to the champion of the Reformation, invests the old building with fresh charms.

Next to Auerbach's cellar in point of associations is the castle of Pleissenburg, at the south-east angle of the city walls; a citadel which withstood the attacks of Tilly during the Thirty Years'

CASTLE OF PLEISSENBURG.

War, and held out for weeks after the city had succumbed to its unmerciful foe. I remember standing on the observatory at the top of the Pleissenburg tower some years ago, and by the aid of a guide tracing out in the broad flat landscape all round the chief points of interest connected with the *Völkerschlacht*, or Battle of the Nations, fought in the month of October, 1813, one of the largest, longest, and bloodiest actions in the annals of war, and fought with the most momentous results, for it decided the fate of Europe—checking the ambitious career of Napoleon, and lifting up Germany out of the dust. Murray's Guide Book dwells on it at length; but, in the thirteenth edition, says nothing of associations gathering round that same castle, and weaving into the story of the citadel the name which is the pole-star of our present travels. It was in this very Pleissenburg that the Leipzig disputation was held.

When Luther, as described in a former paper, was at Augsburg, —where, by-the-bye, his acquaintance with Auerbach began—he came into friendly contact with Dr. Eck, or Eckius,—a man of learning and logical acuteness, a master of scholastic wrangling— strongly attached to the Popedom, but not out of all sympathy with Martin in the earlier portion of his career. An eminent scholastic, Andrew Rudolph Bodenstein, surnamed Carlstadt, a name by which he is best known in history, agreed with Luther on certain points and published a number of theses, or propositions, some of them favourable to the Reformer's views. The propositions were not approved by Eck, and, in some respects, they appear not to have been approved by Luther, for he agreed at Augsburg that a debate should be held by Eck and Carlstadt to settle the differences between them. But Eck, in bracing himself up for a conflict with Carlstadt, began to threaten Luther as well—conduct which the latter resented with all the vehemence of his fiery nature, calling him an " animalculum of fame," full of stupid sycophancy. The dispute which was to be held by Eckius with Carlstadt branched out into a further dispute with Luther; and at length these three theologians publicly discussed the questions which had set them at variance.

The question as to the place of discussion was of considerable importance. Wittenberg and Leipzig had by this time—the year 1519—become the strongholds of two contending powers, the Reformation and Rome. Frederick, the Elector of Saxony, looked with pride on the extending fame of Wittenberg, and agreed with Luther in ecclesiastical tendencies; and had the disputation been appointed to be held there, the champions of reform would have been supported by a sympathetic population as well as a sympathetic prince. On the other hand, Duke George of Saxony, with Dresden as his capital, looked on Leipzig, with its university, as the ecclesiastical centre of his dominions; and as he threw the weight of his influence into the papal scale—though he was not free from some touches of liberal feeling—he was favourable to the impending debate being held there, where Eckius particularly desired it should take place for the honour both of the university and the Duke. The point was carried in favour of Leipzig.

There, accordingly, preparations were made for a grand debate in the summer of 1519. Discussions held at public meetings in the present day give no sort of idea of the discussions of the sixteenth century; and however important and imposing they may have been in England at that period, Germany bore away the palm of magnificence and effect in such proceedings. They have been often compared to tournaments, and not without reason: certainly this polemical encounter at Leipzig was conducted under circumstances of splendour which forcibly remind us of the grand array upon a mediæval tilting-ground; and the theses and rules of debate were more elaborate and perplexing than the laws of chivalry, ruling the attack and defence allowed in the lists to knights of old.

The narrative of the opening of the business certainly reads like the story of so many men in armour, with squires and heralds, passing the barriers.

First came Eck into Leipzig on the 21st June, the feast of Corpus Christi, attended by Poliander, "A youth whom he brought with him from Ingolstadt, to write an account of the disputation. All manner of honours were paid to the scholastic Doctor. Arrayed in the robes of the priesthood, and followed by a numerous procession, he traversed the streets of the city on the day of the festival. All pressed to have a glimpse of him :" the theological faculty of the university treated him with distinction ; the city council provided for him a feast.[1]

On the 24th of June, the Feast of St. John, came Carlstadt, riding in a carriage, followed by other chariots containing Duke Barnim of Pomerania, at that time a Wittenberg student and the chosen rector of the university, accompanied by Martin Luther, Philip Melancthon, Nicholas Amsdorf—whose house at Eisenach has been mentioned—and John Lange, Vicar of the Augustinians. Several Doctors of Law—some Masters of Arts—two Licentiates in Theology, and other ecclesiastics, with two hundred students on foot, carrying spears and halberds, closed the procession. One of the wheels of Carlstadt's carriage broke down as he passed St. Paul's Church, and that rather self-important personage had to seek his lodgings on foot: the vehicle containing Luther passed safely onward to its destination.

Duke George of Saxony had the great hall of the Pleissenburg fitted up for the accommodation of the disputants and their friends. Two pulpits were erected facing each other ; one exhibiting the portrait of St. Martin, the other the portrait of St. George ; like a couple of shields bearing the devices of the champions to whom they belonged. There were benches for spectators hung with tapestry and tables for the use of notaries who had to report the discussion.

[1] D'Aubigné, "History of the Reformation," book v., c. ii. Sears, 243.

The 27th of June was fixed for the first meeting. On the morning of that day both parties assembled at the university and proceeded to hear mass at St. Thomas' Church. Then all marched to the Pleissenburg, Duke George and the Duke of Pomerania taking the lead; next came Counts, Abbots, and Knights; last followed the Doctors and their friends, a band of music occupying the rear. In the hall the beautiful hymn "Veni Sancte Spiritus" was sung; Luther's noble voice, we may be sure, rising above the voices of many. Luther, as described by an eye-witness, was of middle size, and had become so lean that you might almost count his bones. He was in the prime of life, and had a clear and sonorous voice. He had the Word of God at his fingers' ends. In conversation he was candid and affable, "had nothing but strict thoughts," and could accommodate himself to society—being pleasant and full of hearty good-humour.

Carlstadt was not so tall as Luther; he was of a dusky complexion, and had a disagreeable utterance. He, notwithstanding possessed, though in a less degree, some of the qualities which distinguished his friend.

Eck was tall and broad-shouldered, and had a strong German voice, "fit for the stage—fit for a public crier." His accentuation was thick, rather than distinct. His mouth, eyes, and countenance gave the impression of his being a soldier or a butcher, rather than a divine. This description proceeds from no friendly pen; and Eck is further painted as slow of comprehension and defective in judgment, and as a man of inconceivable impudence; but he is credited with an excellent memory, which enabled him to heap passage on passage from the Fathers, with a perseverance which must have been perplexing to his opponents.

We cannot follow the debate throughout its manifold windings. Eck and Carlstadt began and carried on a controversy upon free will, which lasted a whole week.

LUTHER AT LEIPZIG. *From the Painting by Schnorr.*

On the 4th of July a discussion ensued between Luther and Eck; not, it may be said, according to previous arrangement, but Luther could not and would not hold his peace, and from the beginning prepared himself for the discussion. His interest in the controversy was intense, and his desire to speak irrepressible, the more so, in consequence of the unexpected turn which in some respects the discussion took. He had indeed promised to be silent, but only on condition that Eck should not attack any of his published propositions. In the end, he considered that Eck had attacked him whilst dealing with Carlstadt, and therefore felt himself released from his promise. It appears impossible that Luther could be a mute spectator, when we find him in the month of May writing to Spalatin in the following terms: "This matter, if it be of God, shall not have an end, except that as the disciples and friends of Christ forsook Him, so all my friends forsake me; and the truths which saves with its own right hand, not mine, nor that of any other man, shall be left to itself alone." "If I perish, nothing will perish with me." "I am unhappy because I fear I am not worthy to suffer and to be put to death for such a cause. That felicity will be reserved for better men, not for such a vile sinner as I am." "Death will certainly come at some time." Verily he carried his life in his hand, and could say with Paul, to reforming compeers, "I protest by your rejoicing which I have in Christ Jesus, I die daily."

When Luther met Eck in debate they occupied two pulpits, Luther carrying a nosegay in his hand. They continued until the 8th of the month, debating upon the supremacy of the Pope, purgatory, indulgences, and absolution. When Eck had propounded his theses as to the Church and its visible head, Luther replied, "The Head of the Church militant is Jesus Christ Himself, and not a man. This I hold in virtue of God's own testimony.

[1] The day of the month is not given. The letter may be found in Luther's *Briefe*, i. 260.

Christ, saith the Scriptures, must reign till He hath put all enemies under His feet. Let us not listen then to those who would confine Christ to the Church triumphant in heaven. His reign is a reign of faith. We see not our Head, yet we have Him." With such incisive words Luther, at one stroke, cut through sophistries touching the Pope's headship or viceregency.

One important issue of the disputation was that Luther was led by it into clearer views of the Headship of Christ, and the unscriptural and irrational character of papal pretensions. He had, notwithstanding the expressions he had occasionally used, been unwilling to go any great length in opposition to the supremacy of the Pope. But men are trained by the discipline of circumstances, and are ultimately brought to conclusions latent in premises which they took up without seeing at first what they contained. So Luther was trained; so he was led on step by step; his eyes were opened as he contended with Eckius, and he began to see further into the truth of Christ's Lordship over the Church than he had formerly discerned. Another result was the impression made on George of Anhalt—a Leipzig student, twelve years old, who sat on one of the tapestried benches, listening to the Wittenberg professor, and who in his riper years came forward boldly on the side of the Reformation; other students also, received into their minds seeds of truth which never perished.

Two further incidents deserve attention. Three or four days after the disputation had been begun, Luther was requested by the Duke of Pomerania to preach in the castle chapel; but the place was too confined; the overflowing congregation adjourned to the hall of the Pleissenburg. Luther preached on the topic of the day—the grace of God and the power of Peter; and popularised the arguments against Rome which in scholastic guise he had maintained in debate with Eckius—much, of course, to the annoyance of that divine, who forthwith delivered four sermons in reply to Luther. The parish pulpits, opened to his antagonist, were closed against him; no opportunity of presenting a rejoinder was given; and Luther complained not only of the unfriendliness of the Leipzig clergy, but of the Leipzig burgesses also.

Melancthon, as we have seen, accompanied Luther to this contest; he aided him, too, by his learning and wisdom; but they were different men, a fact of which Luther was conscious. "I was born," he says, " to engage in earnest struggles on the field of battle with priests and with demons. Hence my writings are full of war and storm. It is necessary that I uproot the stocks and trunks, clear away the thorns and brushwood, fill up the swamps and sloughs. I am the rough woodman whose office it is to open up the highways and to smooth the roads. But the master of arts, Philip, advances with the utmost calmness and gentleness; he tills the ground and plants it out; he joyfully sows and waters according to the gifts that God has so liberally bestowed on him."

Luther was more at home amidst the storm of a public debate than his gentle friend. That friend did not approve of the way in which the controversy was carried on. He did not imagine much good would come out of it. "One can't but wonder," he remarked, "when thinking of the violence that has been shown in treating of all these things. How was any good to be drawn from them? The Spirit of God loves retirement and silence—it is there that He enters into the hearts of men. The Bride of Christ does not remain in the streets and crossings, but she conducts her Bridegroom into her mother's house." Most true, there must be controversy; the Church needs her Luthers no less than her Melancthons; but there can be no doubt that quiet, patient reflection on God's Word, in the spirit of prayer, is the best key to unlock the secrets of the gospel. A translator of D'Aubigné's "History of the Reformation" appropriately cites in this connection two verses from a beautiful hymn by Cowper:—

"The calm retreat, the silent shade,
  With prayer and praise agree,
And seem by Thy sweet bounty made
  For those who follow Thee.

"There if Thy Spirit touch the soul,
  And grace her mean abode,
Oh, with what peace, and joy, and love,
  She communes with her God!"

We meet with Luther again at Leipzig in May, 1539, just after the death of Duke George. His brother Henry, a Protestant, claimed the dukedom, and exercised authority. His first act was to promote Protestantism by inviting Luther to preach in his dominions, "the man of all others most detested by his predecessor."

The Reformer preached in St. Nicholas Church. "There was such a crowd that all the spaces about the pillars and railings and passages were full, and many stood out of doors and heard him through the windows."[1] Contemporary records, with some exaggeration, declare that most of the citizens, in a single day, were converted to the Protestant faith.[2] Luther had predicted what appeared at the time a strange event: "I shall one day preach God's word in Leipzig."

[1] Sears, "Luther," p. 406.
[2] See Waddington's "History of the Reformation," vol. iii., p. 291.

X.

Diet of Worms.

MANY a year has passed and gone since, returning home from Switzerland by the Rhine, in a steamer which then plied between Strasburg and Mayence, I first saw the twin towers of Worms Cathedral at a distance. There they stand, about a mile from the river, on the fertile level which stretches away from the low banks, rich in romantic associations; for all round Worms lies the Wonnegau, or land of joy, a spot which inspired the lays of the Minnesänger. It is in part the scene of the stories of the Nibelungenlied; and opposite the landing-place, by the Rheinischer Hof, is the island of Rosengarten, which, according to the legend, was "some seven miles in circuit, fenced only by a silk thread." But not of mediæval myths was I thinking when the old reddish-looking twin towers first met my view; but of him with whom the place has now, for three centuries and a half, been associated; and then arose an earnest desire to visit the homes and haunts of Martin Luther, a desire which at intervals, during a quarter of a century or so, has been richly gratified. Circumstances, at the time, did not permit my exploring the old German city, which seemed to beckon me on so temptingly ; but a few years afterwards I was enabled to gratify my curiosity respecting it; then and since, with a rare enjoyment, have I rambled through the streets, and outside the walls, thinking of the memorable visit paid to Worms by the great Reformer in the spring of 1521.

It was late on an August evening that I and a dear friend entered within the gates, and were conveyed from the railway station to an old-fashioned inn,—not indeed so venerable as to wear the honours of between three and four centuries,—but yet sufficiently antique to be in keeping with the object of our pilgrimage. After the fatigues of a long day's journey, sleep was most welcome, and we were rather too soon disturbed in the morning by the bells of a neighbouring church ; yet bells carry a tone which comes from memory's land ; the spirits of the belfry always pour out music of the past rather than of the future, and their fingers ever point behind, not before—so the bells at Worms, that pleasant sunny morning, chimed in with the purpose of our visit, and struck a keynote in harmony with the employment of the day.

Of course our attention was directed to the sights renowned in guide-books—the markets ; the Place St. André, the Rathhaus, and certain churches, especially the Domkirche, or Cathedral, a grand Romanesque building, the twin towers of which have just been mentioned. Chapels and sculptures, and a charming pointed portal of the fifteenth century mirrored themselves in my mind more or less distinctly; yet I confess that what was uppermost when we were actually in the place, remains uppermost in imagination still ; and mediæval forms of architecture chiefly serve now, as they did then, to throw a fitting background into pictures of the man who came there to vindicate the rights of conscience—to do battle with deadly errors, and, on the side of God's own Word, to

CITY OF WORMS.

fling down before princes and potentates, bishops and priests, the gauntlet of the Reformation.

At an early hour we took a walk to Pfiffligheim, not very far from the town, along a road bordered by trees laden with fruit, and dividing, without any hedgerows, the public thoroughfare from the far-spreading and well-cultivated fields of the German farmers, then waving with promises of a rich summer crop. There are hours in life when, by a happy combination of weather, scenery, circumstances, society, health, and buoyant spirits, an Elysian kind of lot befalls even common mortals; cares are thrown off, troubles are forgotten, the air breathes peace, the sun pours down gladness, the birds chirp merry strains, and the voice of friendship is heard above them in tones of sympathy which enhances the beauty of every wild flower, of every green tree, of every bit of woodland, every stretch of cornfield, and every fleck of cloud floating up in the azure sky. So it was that morning, as we walked on the road towards Oppenheim.

Luther passed Oppenheim on his way to the Diet. His letters enable us to follow him through his journey from Wittenberg to Worms. He paused at Leipzig, Naumberg, Weimar, Erfurt, Gotha, and Frankfort, travelling, at least part of the way, in a waggon with leather curtains. At Frankfort there stands at one corner of the Dom Platz an old house bearing his name, with the inscription: "In silentio et spe erit fortitudo vestra." There probably he tarried on this occasion, certainly at the time he found that in quietness and confidence was the secret of his strength. "All the way from Eisenach," he says in a letter, already noticed, written at Frankfort, April 14, "I have been ill, and am so now to a degree I have not known before. I understand that the Emperor Charles has issued his mandate for the purpose of terrifying me, but Christ liveth, and I will enter Worms in spite of all the gates of hell, and all the powers of the air."

Some years after I took that walk I visited Oppenheim, and

tarried there during an autumnal afternoon and evening, being entertained at a goodly castle which was surrounded by flower gardens, and commanded a magnificent view of the Rhine. I revelled in the charms of the landscape; and the pleasure was enhanced by the hospitality of German friends familiar with the neighbourhood, one of them an occupant of the delightful spot. I knew that Luther had tarried at Oppenheim on his way to Worms, but I did not know that his resting-place could be identified. What then was my gratification when a lady at the Castle, a friend of many years, undertook to be my cicerone, and to show me the house where Luther lodged. I was conducted down the hill into a street, the principal one in the town, where stood a good-sized hostelry of the true German type, with rows of windows running across the front. The *Ritter*, I think, is the sign. "There," said my informant, "Luther rested on his road to Worms; and it is a local tradition, that in that room," pointing to an upper window, "he slept, and being left-handed, so people here say, he opened the casement in his own fashion, and that fashion is often followed here in memory of him." This, of course, is one of the welcome waifs and strays one likes to pick up, without vouching for the truth of the story, and as the inside of the inn presented nothing remarkable, I hastened to see whatever else of interest there might be in Oppenheim.

Two objects I well remember: first, the ruins of the Castle of Landskron, once an Imperial Castle; and secondly, the Church of St. Catherine, of which an interesting History was offered by the person who conducted us over the building. Part is in ruins, part is in tolerable repair. The towers are of the twelfth century; the nave, of much later date, with painted glass—almost perfect—is exceedingly elegant. There is a rose window full of elaborate tracery, and there are tombstones four hundred years old. Amongst armorial bearings which remain in this beautiful edifice, are those of the family of Sickengen, who belonged to the neighbourhood, and were connected with the Church. Here we get on the Luther track again. Franz of Sickengen was one of those knights errant who terrified the people of Worms and Frankfort; but he befriended the Reformers, and figures in the history of early Protestantism. He sympathised with it, if not on its spiritual, yet on its temporal and political side. He disliked the priesthood, and preferred the secular to the ecclesiastical power. In his rude castle of Ebernburg, not far from Oppenheim—nor from Kreuznach on the Vale of the Nahr Railway—he entertained Melancthon, Bucer, and Œcolampadius. There also the famous Ulric von Hutten wrote some of his works. When Luther was at Oppenheim, at the Ritter hostelry as I suppose, a troop of horsemen came dashing into the town, led by Martin Bucer, then on a visit to Sickengen. "These cavaliers," said the Reformer, "belong to Franz of Sickengen. He has sent me to conduct you to his castle." Franz was then looked up to as a protector. "You two together," says a correspondent of Ulric von Hutten, after mentioning Franz, " will be the thunder and lightning to crush the monster of Rome." Merle d'Aubigné[1] represents an artful plan, as laid by Luther's adversaries to entrap him on his approach to Worms, and he considers that Bucer was a simple-minded instrument, misled and employed by them to accomplish their mischievous purpose. The authorities cited by the graphic historian do not appear to me sufficient to substantiate his view. Luther was travelling under an Imperial safe-conduct to the city of the Diet, and friends questioned the wisdom of relying on that document, seeing that a safe-conduct in the case of Huss had been broken. Enemies also were found who said the Emperor Charles was not bound to keep his word with heretics. Hence the warning sent to Luther may be more probably regarded as originating with friends, not foes.

It was at Oppenheim that Luther received from Spalatin a message, telling him not to think of entering Worms. It would be so very dangerous. The grandees of Germany were there assembling

[1] "History of the Reformation."

in conclave. Ecclesiastical as well as political affairs awaited settle-

LUTHER HOUSE AT FRANKFORT.

ment. Luther's books and theses and manifold defiances of Rome were troubling the empire from end to end, creating sympathy in the minds of some, arousing indignation and revenge in the minds of others. Charles v. was himself at Worms, and had written to the Elector to bring Luther with him to answer for himself before the world and the Church. Come he must. "Come I will," said Martin. "I will be carried there sick, sooner than not come at all. Without doubt I am called of God, if called by the Emperor. He lives who preserved the three men in the fiery furnace. He will preserve me." It was not the policy of Rome that he should come. Rome having already excommunicated him, only wished the excommunication to be carried out, and the troublesome monk to be silenced.

"The papists," says Luther, "do not wish that I may come, but simply that I may be condemned and destroyed." But the Emperor was disposed, especially through the influence and persuasion of the Elector of Saxony, to whom he was under obligation, to have Luther brought before him and the representatives of his German dominions. Intrigues, manœuvres, and schemes were the order of the day, and made his appearance before the Diet, though at the Emperor's command, very perilous. There were plenty of laymen and priests who would have liked to get the troublesome Augustinian into their hands; and who could tell what would happen to him if he ventured into Worms, as John Huss ventured into Constance? So Spalatin sent to the traveller, on his reaching Oppenheim, saying, "Come no farther." The whole world has heard his answer over a thousand times, and somehow never seems tired of hearing it; for it is one of those trumpet-tongued utterances which wake up in the souls of all who are worth anything a sympathetic response. Nobody who admires what is brave and good, but is ready across the ages to cheer the champion —as across the ages there come the words, "If there were as many devils in Worms as there are tiles on the house-tops, I would go thither." So on he went.

At Pfiffligheim, on the road to Oppenheim, there stands a tall thin-looking elm, called the Lutherbaum, or Luther's tree. According to one account he here saw a peasant planting elms. "Give me one of them," he said, "and I will place it in the earth. God grant my doctrine may flourish like the branch of this tree." That tree flourished long, according to all accounts, but was cut down in 1811. The present one is believed to occupy the place of it. Murray's Handbook speaks as if he used his well-known words of defiance at this very spot. That was not literally the case; but the spirit of the utterance must have been in him as he drove up to the spot, and braced himself for the last short stage to the city, which many of his friends thought would be a lion's den. God might save him as he did Daniel, but the prudent said it would be tempting Providence. How the old story came out with the most vivid colouring—how plainly could we see him, in an open Saxon waggon, on solid wooden wheels, with the monk whom he calls his brother, and Nicholas Amsdorf, and Von Suaven, a Pomeranian nobleman; the imperial herald on horseback, with the imperial escutcheon before, and Justas Jonas and his servant behind! It was at ten o'clock, an eye-witness states, that the procession approached the city. It was about that time that we stood under the elm-tree, and imagined the scene passing before us. As we returned to Worms along the dusty road,—when there were fewer buildings outside the town than there are now, and the brown towers of the cathedral rose over the city amidst a bright blue sky—and met the farmers' carts, and thought of Luther, we could see the house-roofs of the city peering above the horizon—streets of tiles, like crowds of foes. What an illustration of his words! "Never mind," he virtually said, "I will fear no evil; Thy rod and Thy staff they comfort me." Sometimes men wonder at their courage, thinking of it afterwards. Luther did. "I was then a fearless man; I dreaded nothing. God can inspire a man with so much daring. I do not know that I should be so confident now." It is believed by some that it was on his way to Worms that he composed his famous hymn, *Ein' feste Burg ist unser*

FACSIMILE OF THE ORIGINAL OF "EIN' FESTE BURG."
From the "Luther Codex," lately discovered, dating from the year 1530.

A safe stronghold our God is still,
  A trusty shield and weapon;
He'll help us clear from all the ill
  That hath us now o'ertaken.
The ancient Prince of hell
Hath risen with purpose fell;
Strong mail of craft and power
He weareth in this hour,
On earth is not his fellow.

With force of arms we nothing can,
  Full soon were we down-ridden;
But for us fights the proper Man,
  Whom God Himself hath bidden.
Ask ye, Who is this same?
Christ Jesus is His name,
The Lord Zebaoth's Son,
He and no other one
Shall conquer in the battle.

And were this world all devils o'er,
  And watching to devour us,
We lay it not to heart so sore,
  Not they can o'erpower us.
And let the prince of ill
Look grieved as e'er he will,
He harms us not a whit.
For why? His doom is writ,
A word shall quickly slay him.

God's word, for all their craft and force,
  One moment will not linger,
But, spite of hell, shall have its course,
  'Tis written by His finger.
And though they take our life,
Goods, honour, children, wife,
Yet is their profit small;
These things shall vanish all,
The city of God remaineth.

Translated by Carlyle.

Gott. Thomas Carlyle says, "Luther wrote this song in a time of blackest threatenings, which, however, could in no wise become a time of despair." In those tones, rugged, broken as they are, do we not recognise the accent of that summoned man (summoned not by Charles V., but by God Almighty also), who answered his friend's warning in this wise, "Were there as many devils in Worms as there are roof tiles, I would on"? Michelet, an inferior authority, calls the hymn the *Marseillaise* of the Reformation, and states, with a characteristic aim at effect, that Luther arose in the chariot, and began to sing, as the bell towers of Worms came in sight, the words and the music having been improvised two days before at Oppenheim. But according to a writer who describes the castle of Coburg, in an interesting folio of drawings by the late Mr. Morison (executed at the suggestion of the lamented Prince Consort), the hymn was composed years afterwards in the castle of Coburg. Perhaps the two accounts can be reconciled. May not the germ of the noble psalm have been first conceived on the road to Worms, then gradually wrought into a more perfect form of words and music, and finally written in the old fortress as we have it now? The hymn embodies Luther's spirit, both when present at the Diet of Worms, and when at a distance watching the Diet of Augsburg.

He entered the city about noon, "just as people sat down to dinner. When the watchman on the church tower blew his trumpet everybody crowded into the streets to see the monk. He sat in the open waggon, which the Council of Wittenberg had lent him for the journey, in the cowl of his order."[1] More than two thousand people escorted him to his lodgings. The inn at which Luther alighted is by some authors called the *Deutscher Hof.* There quarters had been provided for him by the Elector, there also were lodged the imperial marshals and two noblemen of the Elector's court.

I inquired after this hostelry on my last visit to Worms, and

[1] Ranke's "History of the Reformation," vol. i., p. 533.

was informed by the landlord of the Alter Kaiser, that there exists no inn of the name just mentioned, and that the house where Luther lodged had been pulled down. This did not satisfy me, and on further inquiry I learned from an intelligent Scotch gardener that the house stood on the Hardt Gasse, to the south-west of the cathedral. After some trouble, I discovered in that street an open spot where a building had recently stood, which I learned had been used as a casino, and was a Maltese house bearing the name of the White Cross. This site, a person living in the street affirmed to be, according to tradition, that on which stood the house occupied by Luther during the Diet: but I had no means of ascertaining what its appearance was.

Whatever the accommodation afforded might be, it is stated that for some hours after his arrival he was allowed to retire and rest himself; but the spring evening had scarcely begun to close in, when people of all sorts, including nobles, knights, priests, and common citizens, pressed into the hotel to see him—some from curiosity, some from kindliness. The Landgrave Philip of Hesse squeezed his hand as he bid him good night, saying, if his cause was good, God would be with him. It was the commencement of a lasting friendship.

We may conclude how troubled was his sleep in the inn from the well-known interjections he was heard to utter, before he appeared amongst his friends next morning. Mathesius has preserved them in his " Life of Luther." " O Almighty and everlasting God, how strong is the world! How little do men put their trust in Thee! . . . . If I turn my eyes to the world, all is over with me: for the die is cast, and my condemnation is pronounced. O God! O God! O Thou my God! Stand by me against the world's reason and wisdom. For Thou must do it—Thou alone. It is not my cause, but Thine own. . . . . I could fain live out my days in quietness, without struggle and perplexity. But Thine is the cause, O Lord, and it is righteous and eternal. Therefore stand by me, Thou righteous and eternal God! I put not my trust in any man... Dost Thou not hear me, O my God? Art Thou dead? No! Thou canst not die. Thou only hidest Thy face. Oh tell me, hast Thou not chosen me for this work? I know that Thou hast... Be Thou upon my side, O God, for the honour of Thy dear Son Jesus Christ... Though my body, which is the work of Thy hands, should perish, yea, be torn to pieces, ... my soul is Thine, and belongs to Thee, and shall abide with Thee for ever and ever. Amen."

Even men who are little accustomed to pray will pour out their hearts before God in a time of trouble; how much more men like Luther, to whom prayer has become a second nature! His petitions were pitched in a key of agonizing earnestness, like that indicated by the great Lord of prayer when He said: "The kingdom of heaven suffereth violence, and the violent take it by force." The very day the Reformer thus prayed, he received a letter at Worms, from the eccentric Ulric von Hutten, who began with the words: "The Lord hear thee in the day of trouble! the name of the God of Jacob defend thee! Send thee help from the sanctuary, and strengthen thee out of Zion! Grant thee according to thine own heart, and fulfil all thy counsel!" It was like an answer from heaven. Such passages of Scripture were the staff and stay of Martin Luther in the hour of conflict. He had been wrestling with the Angel of the Covenant, and that day at Worms felt how the Great Unseen was blessing him there.

At four o'clock a herald came to the inn, to summon him to appear before the Emperor. The crowd was immense; the public thoroughfares were blocked up; windows were filled with faces; men and boys scrambled up to the house-tops. It was necessary to conduct the object of this curiosity by a back way through private passages, to the place where the Diet had assembled. Where was that place? The prevalent tradition amongst the townspeople points to the Bishop's palace, destroyed by the French in the year 1689, and, after being rebuilt, destroyed again by the French in 1794.

On the north side of the Dom is a red stone wall belonging to the old Bishop's Hof, and the external wall of the Dom opposite indicates, between them, the existence once of a building there now pulled down. In an ancient map of Worms, I noticed a covered corridor connecting the palace with the cathedral, just at that point. The site of the episcopal residence is now a beautiful garden, where I met with the intelligent Scotch gardener, who not only directed attention to his charming plants and shrubs, but also to objects of interest connected with the vanished buildings, at the same time adopting the tradition just now cited. He also showed a model of the palace as it appeared after its reconstruction in 1719, presenting a long façade, with a bay in the middle and with wings, an arcade running round, and dormer windows jutting out on the roof. The second palace is said to have resembled the first, and of this last building a vault or cellar still remains. Contrary to the town tradition, D'Aubigné in his "History of the Reformation," and Sears in his "Life of Luther," speak of the Town or Guild Hall as the place where the Diet was held ; and Michelet, in his "Life of the Reformer," represents Luther as stating the Town Hall to have been the place of assembly.[1] But an examination of the original account, given in Luther's works, settles the question the other way. Luther in the notice of his first audience does not specify any place at all,[2] and in the account of his second audience he only uses the general expression of "*Saal*," or "Hall."[3] But Spalatin, in his description of the first audience, distinctly mentions "*the Bischofs Hof*" as the scene of the memorable transaction. Spalatin was not likely to be mistaken.[4]

[1] Life of Luther by Michelet, translated by Hazlitt, Bohn's Edition, p. 82. No reliance can be placed on his quotations in critical instances, or to his references at any time.

[2] Luther's Works, Walch's Edition, vol. xv., col. 2231.

[3] *Ibid.*, col. 2233.

[4] Luther's Works, Walch's Edition, vol. xv., col. 2232. Spalatin has, "auf die Pfalz

When the Diet opened in the palace, access to the hall was thronged. With difficulty Luther got towards the door, when he felt a tap on his shoulder, and heard a friendly voice—an old soldier's, George of Freundsberg—exclaiming, " Little monk, thou art marching to a battle such as neither I nor any other general ever fought. If thou art sure of having right on thy side, press on in the name of God, and fear nothing. God will not forsake you." There were present the Emperor, six Electors, an Archduke, twenty-seven Dukes, two Landgraves, five Margraves, and numerous Counts, Archbishops, and Bishops. The galleries, doors, and windows of the hall were crowded. Amongst the noblest there were some who spoke to the bold monk of Saxony in tones of encouragement. One said, "Fear not them which kill the body, but are not able to kill the soul." "When," said another. "ye shall be brought before kings, the Spirit of your Father will speak in you."

His first appearance amounted to little more than a matter of form. He was asked whether the books published in his name were his; he answered in the affirmative. He was also asked whether he would retract what he had written; he replied that he must beg truce of his imperial Majesty before he answered so important a question. The Emperor allowed him one day for consideration. Luther returned to his hotel, and sat down and wrote to Cuspianus, imperial councillor, "I have stood before the Emperor and his brother, and have been asked whether I would retract what I have written. I have acknowledged the books to be mine, and have promised to answer to-morrow respecting retractation. Verily I will not retract one jot, Christ being my helper."

---

oder des Bischofs Hof." "Pfalz," when used of a building, is very much the same as our "palace." Since writing the above I find Köstlin states that the hall in the palace was the place for holding Diets, and hence it came to be called the *Rath-haus*, or Council Hall. This no doubt has caused confusion as to the locality of the Diet.

In the course of that day there was an uproar in Worms. Spaniards quarrelled with the citizens. Copies of Luther's book on the Babylonish captivity were found torn to pieces, whereupon the people who sympathized in the Reformation avenged this insult and attacked the offenders.

At four o'clock next day, Luther was brought before the Diet again, amidst crowds as before ; and as the afternoon grew dark, torches were brought into the hall, heightening the solemn aspect of the assembly by the lights and shadows thrown over the building. There he stood and spoke to this effect :—that he had composed books on different subjects, some of which even his adversaries approved ; that he had also written against the Papacy, in which he was supported by the complaints of God-fearing men, and to retract what he had freely stated on the subject would be to increase evils widely complained of ; that he had also published works against private persons, perhaps with too much acrimony ; but he could revoke none of his positions, unless they were proved to be untrue : in that case he would commit his writings to the flames.

Luther spoke in German ; but, upon being requested to do so, repeated his speech in Latin. Then, after further pressure on the point of retractation, he uttered the never-to-be-forgotten sentence, 'Unless I be convicted of error by the Scriptures, or by powerful reasons, neither can I nor will I dare to retract anything, for my conscience is bound to God's word, and it is neither safe nor right to go against conscience. *Hier stehe ich : ich kann nicht anders : Gott helfe mir. Amen.* (Here I stand : I can do no otherwise : God help me.)

Luther was as bold as Paul before Agrippa, and was filled with the same consciousness of Divine truth as the apostle was, when he defied men and angels to preach any other gospel than that which God had taught him. There were those who were slow to take Luther's answer. He was reminded of the course adopted towards obstinate heretics. Still he said, "God help me! I can retract nothing." Called back, he was asked to qualify his declaration. "No," said he, "I have no other answer than that have given."

Leaving the hall, people shouted, "Is he going to prison?" "No," he answered, "to my hotel." There Luther was accosted by a footman of the Duke of Brunswick, who brought him a tankard of German beer, such as Luther liked. "As Duke Erick has this day remembered me," said he, after a good draught of the beverage, "so may our Lord Jesus Christ remember him in the hour of his last conflict." The story goes that the Duke on his death-bed remembered this, when a page read to him out of the Gospel, "Whosoever shall give you a cup of water to drink in My name, because ye belong to Christ, verily I say unto you, he shall not lose his reward."

"The Rhine ought to receive his ashes, as it received a century ago the ashes of John Huss," said certain zealots who attended the Diet of Worms; and even Charles said afterwards that it was one of the greatest blunders of his life to let Luther off as he did; but the idea of violating the imperial safe-conduct, as in the case of Huss, the great scandal of the fifteenth century, horrified some of the princes of Germany, and they would not hear of its being repeated in the sixteenth.

From day to day distinguished men crossed the threshold of Luther's inn at Worms to see and talk with him. The sympathy on one hand seems more wonderful than the animosity on the other. The Archbishop of Treves sent for him at the archiepiscopal lodgings; the Chancellor of Baden strove to win over the Saxon Reformer. "Commit yourself to the Emperor's judgment, and don't be afraid." "My conscience hangs on God's word," returned Luther. "Then, if I rightly understand," rejoined the Chancellor, "you do not acknowledge any authority but Scripture?" "Precisely so."

Afterwards we find Luther in good humour supping with the Archbishop at his lodgings. A story is told on the authority of an eye-witness (but Luther does not mention it) that a wine-glass fell to pieces in his hand. "There must have been poison in it," thought his friends. "It never was meant for me," said Luther himself; "the glass went to shivers from having been plunged in cold water when washed." And so he turned aside the suspicion, for which, under the circumstances, there really was no ground.

An imperial message at last reached the hotel, commanding Luther to depart, but giving a safe-conduct for twenty days. At ten o'clock he left with his friends. Twenty gentlemen on horseback surrounded the vehicle in which he rode, till he had passed out of the gates into the open country.

His presence was troublesome to his enemies, and when the twenty days' safe-conduct should expire, there was no saying what might be done with him. He had been outlawed by the Diet. The bill for that purpose was drawn up May 25th, and signed the next day; but it was dated as far back as the 8th to conceal the fact of its being prepared after several members of the Diet had left.[1]

The papal nuncio, Aleander, writing from Worms, discloses the disturbed state of public opinion, at the time divided in one respect, united in another; as he remarks, "The whole of Germany is in an uproar, nine persons out of ten are for Luther, and even the tenth does not trouble himself about the edict which condemns him; but all wish for the destruction of the Roman Church, everybody cries for a council! a council!!"[2]

Luther left Worms on Friday, April 26th, and the same day Gaspar Contarini, the Venetian ambassador, says in one of his letters:—

[1] We learn this rom Pallavicino, in his History of the Council of Trent.
[2] "Etude Historique sur le Concile de Trente." Premier partie, 1545-62. Paris, 1874.

LUTHER'S MONUMENT AT WORMS.

"During the night of the day on which the Emperor dismissed Luther, a writing was placarded on the doors of the cathedral, whereby four hundred nobles and persons innumerable of inferior grade threatened the opponents of Luther; and defied them to battle, making especial mention of the Bishop of Mayence, whom they vituperated greatly.

"Luther's books are sold publicly in Worms, although the Pope and the Emperor, who is on the spot, have prohibited them."[1]

. In the summer of 1869 was inaugurated the elaborate monument which now adorns the west side of Worms, not far from a remaining portion of the city wall, under which ran the fosse or ditch in Luther's time. It commemorates the Reformation, exhibiting a number of celebrities connected with that event. At the four corners stand Frederick the Wise, Philip the Magnanimous, Philip Melancthon, and John Reuchlin ; and between these figures on three sides are emblems of Augsburg with a palm-branch, Magdeburg mourning over her desolate hearths, and Spires offering her famous protest. Luther surmounts the pedestal in the middle rising in this emblematical memorial of the Reformation, as he did in actual fact, above all his contemporaries, whether ecclesiastical, literary, or royal.

The British and Foreign Bible Society availed itself of the inauguration, and was permitted by the authorities to erect a stall for the sale of Scriptures, when a continual stream of buyers set in, and there occurred the following incidents, described by the late Rev. Mr. Davies, agent of the Society in Germany.

"One peasant said, pointing to a Bible, 'After all, this is the genuine monument of Martin Luther.' Others, 'I promised my family a memento of the festival; this is the best memento, a beautiful copy of Martin Luther's translation of the Holy Bible.' It was singular to see how the enthusiasm became contagious, extending even to the Catholics and Jews. Two women, mother

---

[1] State papers, Venetian correspondence.

and daughter, approached, and looked long at a copy of Luther's Bible, talking earnestly the while. Then they went away. They returned again and looked at the volume." "Our colporteurs," adds Mr. Davies, "were much too busy to heed them, I therefore advanced, and they at once addressed me and said, 'We are Catholics, but we think it a shame not to read Luther's Bible ; for, after all, it is the Book of God, and it was Martin Luther who again gave it to the people.' I encouraged them by all means to carry out their purpose, and they at once advanced to the table and paid for the book.

"One interesting feature of our table was a large folio Bible of the year 1541, printed in Wittenberg.

"I had it placed on the table because I thought it would interest the theological public. It lay open, and on it a pearl Bible, a pocket edition. The contrast in size showed in a striking light the difference between the sixteenth and nineteenth centuries in regard to the printing of the Scriptures. In sending the Bible to Worms I thought of nothing more. But for the peasantry it turned out to have almost a religious significance. One woman, for example, approached the table, and asked what the Bible meant. She was told that Bible was printed in Wittenberg while Martin Luther was still alive, and was carried through the press by the great man himself. She left, and returned, bringing with her her two daughters. She asked to be allowed to put her hand on the venerable book. It was permitted her. She stretched out her hand and reverently put it on the Bible, and burst into tears. In like manner, her daughters imitated her, and all left, weeping from excitement. I once dined at the house of a Geneva banker with a very celebrated English preacher. The conversation turned on Luther. 'I cannot,' said the guest of the day, 'reverence Luther as I ought ; he had no heart.' The remark elicited strong expressions of dissent, and I ventured to say that one of the most indisputable proofs that Luther had a great heart was to be found

CATHEDRAL AT WORMS.

in the fact that he lives as no man before or after him in the heart of the German people. A more telling illustration of this truth could not be imagined than the tears of these three German women on seeing and touching this old folio Bible."

Before quitting Worms one word is due to the cathedral. Except fragments of the city walls, it alone remains of all the buildings which existed at the period of the Diet. The external appearance of the structure must have been the same then as it is now. It is of red sandstone, Romanesque in style; the eastern aisle going back to the twelfth century, while pointed arches of a later date distinguish the nave. The portal on the south side, richly adorned with sculpture of the fifteenth century, calls forth the admiration of every one, however unskilled in such works of art; and in the chapel of St. Nicholas are relics in stone brought from a destroyed cloister, representing the Annunciation, the Nativity, the genealogical tree of the Virgin, the Descent from the Cross, and the Resurrection. The figures are curious, some of them very good; traces of early German paintings on the walls and piers add to the interest of this portion of the edifice; and there are good specimens of embossed gravestones in the baptistery and chapel near the south portal. The restoration of the nave and choir has been criticised unfavourably, but without reason; and the whole interior, in length 470 feet, lighted through stained glass windows, struck me as very impressive, from its magnitude, harmony, and simplicity. Services according to the Roman Catholic ritual would probably be conducted in this spacious church during the meetings of the Diet; the Emperor and the court, with the Bishops and other ecclesiastical magnates, would attend some of the solemnities, and the Professor of Theology from Wittenberg would most likely also be present; hence his shadow crossed the pavement as I paced the aisles of the venerable fane.

XI.

THE WARTBURG.

THE castle of this name stands on an eminence, girdled by woods, a little to the south of the town of Eisenach. The building is by no means magnificent, nor, on the whole, is it picturesque; but it exhibits Romanesque arcades, which run back to the twelfth century, and these, with other portions of the edifice, invest it with interest. A large amount of money, taste, and skill has been expended upon it of late: about twenty years ago it was a mere ruin, it is now in such a restored condition that the interior presents corridors, halls, and banqueting-rooms, radiant with frescoed walls, richly coloured ceilings, and polished floors. A curious armoury preserves suits as old as the fourteenth or thirteenth century—some worn by the early lords of the castle and domain. The place is redolent of mediæval taste, chivalry, and romance, so far as the spirit of such things can be revived in the nineteenth century. I do not know many spots where a few hours can be so delightfully spent on a bright summer's day.

There are two ascents to it—one a broad footpath leading directly up to the quaint, low-browed gateway; the other a long winding carriage road, terminating at the same point; both unfolding to the visitor, as he ascends, a wide-spread landscape, diversified by grassy valleys, thick overhanging woods, fields, gardens, and orchards, intermixed with pretty villas and lodging-houses; the town, with its church towers, nestles at the foot of the castle hill; the mountain forest of Thuringia stretches away in different directions farther than eye can reach; the whole is inexpressibly soothing to a tourist jaded by toil.

The castle is famous for its association with the legendary stories of Elizabeth of Hungary, who, as the bride and wife of Lewis, the Landgrave of Thuringia, lived in the castle, and left it—to die at the age of twenty-four. It is certain that this lady was eminently pious and charitable, according to the ideas of the age in which she lived—the thirteenth century; and her eminence in this respect, combined with her rank, made an impression on posterity which led to the development of her cherished memory in all manner of fictitious forms. The legends of those days were fictions founded on facts, pious and charitable acts being clothed in fanciful forms of supernatural drapery. The taste for fiction in the present day may serve to account for the mental craving of the same kind, five or six hundred years ago. We have been taught to discriminate between the historical and the imaginative, and to require verisimilitude in the latter branch of literature; let us thank God for superiority over our fathers, who had been taught no such discrimination: but surely, whilst we condemn the superstitions and magical elements which were blended with other and better materials in old legendary lore, we ought to make some allowance for generations not at all skilled in historical criticism. The real story of Elizabeth is overgrown with poetical myths and fables; but one traces in them a life filled to overflowing " with unseen, untold joys and sorrows, with pangs and struggles such as then haunted the unreasoning minds of women, distracted between their earthly duties and affections and their heavenward aspirations, as if this world were not God's world and His care, no less than that other world." Count Montalembert, Charles Kingsley, and Mrs. Jameson have made modern readers familiar with the stories of St. Elizabeth—that which is identified with the pathway from Eisenach to the castle just described I give in the words of the last author:

"Elizabeth, in the absence of her husband," says Mrs. Jameson, "daily visited the poor who dwelt in the suburbs of Eisenach, and in the huts of the neighbouring valleys. One day, during a severe winter, she left her castle with a single attendant, carrying in the skirts of her robe a supply of bread, meat, and eggs, for a certain poor family; and as she was descending the frozen and slippery path, her husband, returning from the chase, met her bending under the weight of her charitable burden. 'What dost thou here, my Elizabeth?' he said. 'Let us see what thou art carrying away!' and she, confused, and blushing to be so discovered, pressed her mantle to her bosom; but he insisted, and opening her robe, he beheld only red and white roses, more beautiful and fragrant than any that grow on this earth even at summer-tide, and it was now the depth of winter. Then he was about to embrace his wife, but, looking in her face, he was overawed by a supernatural glory which seemed to emanate from every feature, and he dared not touch her: he bade her go on her way, and fulfil her mission; but taking from her lap one of the roses of paradise, he put it in his bosom, and continued to ascend the mountain slowly, with his head declined, and pondering these things in his heart."

Pictorial art has made much of these roses—every traveller reads of them in his guide-book; and the memory of them is preserved in the blushing flowers which abound in the gardens of the neighbourhood.

THE WARTBURG.

But on the heights of the Wartburg the fame of Elizabeth is eclipsed by the fame of Martin Luther, whose eventful story, for nearly a twelvemonth, is interwoven with the castle annals. After quitting Worms, as we have seen, he visited and preached at Eisenach, after which he started, in company with his friend Amsdorf, for a visit to some relations living in a village called

LUTHERSDENKMAL.

Möhra. Whilst he was so engaged, there occurred the friendly capture which made the Wartburg his home for many months.

A few miles to the south of Eisenach lies Altenstein, a charming spot, which may be reached by two roads, commanding views of the Thuringian forest, winding up hill and down dale, the part near Altenstein abounding in oak, lime, beech, and mountain ash; while rural objects, such as groups of charcoal-burners and flocks of geese, amuse the traveller as he drives or walks over this lovely district. Altenstein is an old-fashioned *schloss* or *chateau*, with dark roof, white walls, and green window-shutters, situated on the side of a hill, commanding an extensive prospect, and surrounded with cheerful gardens.

The house is less ancient than Luther's time, but traditions connected with the spot carry us back to times far earlier than his; for it is reported that on a rock in the gardens, surmounted by a cross, Boniface preached to the pagan Saxons. A mile or two from the house there is a little fountain, near a wood, and close to a stone obelisk—commemorating the capture in that romantic situation of the Reformer on his way from the home of his relatives.

Luther expected something of the kind, and was therefore by no means alarmed. In a sandy hollow, at the bend of the road south-east of Altenstein, the Knight von Hund, who resided there, and Berlepsch, governor of the Wartburg, waylaid the traveller, and seized him in his conveyance, then left the road, and conducted him to a beech tree growing near the spring, close to which the monument stands. The beech is called *Luthersbuche*, and the spring *Luthersbrunn*.

An account of this friendly capture is given by Luther himself, in a letter from the Wartburg, addressed to Spalatin, and dated May 14, 1521:

"I went across the forest to visit my kindred, who inhabit that district. Leaving them, and proceeding toward Waltershausen, just after passing the castle of Altenstein I was captured. Amsdorf of necessity knew that some one would save me, but was ignorant of the place of custody. My brother [as he calls his companion, the same who accompanied him to Worms], seeing the knights, leaped in time from the carriage, and without taking leave, proceeded on foot to Waltershausen, which he reached in

LUTHER CARRIED OFF TO THE WARTBURG.

the evening. So here I am, having put off my own attire, and assumed that of a knight, with long hair and long beard, so that you would scarcely know me. Indeed, for some time I have hardly known myself. Now in the enjoyment of Christian liberty, I am free from the laws of the tyrant, though I would (were it the will of God I should suffer for His word) that the Dresden swine [Duke George] should put me to death for preaching. The will of the Lord be done. Farewell, and pray for me."

"What has become of Luther?" was an inquiry throughout Germany and Europe after his disappearance. Various conjectures were afloat; and it is amusing to find in the correspondence of the Venetian ambassador traces of a report very near the truth adopted in influential circles, but soon afterwards completely given up.

"Last evening, at about six p.m.," says Gaspar Contarini, writing from Worms on the 12th of May, "the Cardinal of Mayence sent for the apostolic Francis, and told him that on the day of the Invention of the Cross (the 3rd of May) Friar Martin Luther had been captured by one Hector, a Bohemian, the enemy of the Duke of Saxony, who had followed Luther to Worms, and on the road after his departure. The mode of capture is narrated as follows: Luther, on the day of the Invention of the Cross having preached at a village in the province of Saxony, dismissed the herald who had accompanied him, and in the afternoon, having got into a waggon with one or two persons for the purpose of visiting some of his relations in that neighbourhood, being attacked, *in itinere*, by this Hector, the Bohemian, who made Luther change his apparel, carried him off, whither it is not known."[1]

On the 18th, the same writer says, "In the opinion of intelligent persons, the reported capture of Martin Luther by Hector, the Bohemian, was a fiction, and Luther is safe and sound in Saxony,

[1] Brown's Calendar of Venetian State Papers, vol. iii., p. 121.

and as popular as ever." Again, June 13, Antonio Surian remarks "The capture of Martin Luther has not proved true."[1] What these persons, in common with others, failed to discover was, that the capture was a friendly arrangement, and that the place of retreat was the Wartburg.

Sears, in his "Life of Luther," gives a record of the incidents extracted from the parish records of Schweina, a village which lies at the foot of the hill occupied by the Schloss of Altenstein. I wished to ascertain the accuracy of his statement; accordingly, my friends and I drove down to the village and inquired for the pastor's house. It is close to the church, and the approach of a carriage attracted the attention of the schoolmaster and his boys, who flocked to the windows to see visitors, rather rare in so unfrequented a place. The pastor was most polite: on my making inquiries about the parish register, he procured it, and spreading out the document, pointed to the passage, a translation of which is printed in the book by Dr. Sears: "Saturday, May 4, 1521, between four and five o'clock in the afternoon, Dr. M. Luther passed through the place on his way from Worms, and was taken captive about a mile beyond Altenstein, near Luther's fountain, on the road to Waltershausen, and carried to Wartburg."

Upon my questioning the clergyman as to the author of the record, he stated that from 1614 to 1635, the minister Johannes Hattenbach, a fatherly sort of man,—who has left behind him a patriarchal fame, and who took an interest in historical researches, —having gathered from old neighbours traditions of the parish, carefully preserved this fragment relating to the Saxon Reformer.

The Wartburg, whither Luther was conducted after his capture, has a romantic history. It was built by Ludwig the Leaper between 1067 and 1069, during a severe famine, who, to marry the beautiful Adelaide, wife of the Count Palatine Frederick III., caused him to be murdered whilst hunting. For this base act he

---

[1] Brown's Calendar of Venetian State Papers, vol. iii., p. 121.

was thrown into prison, but escaped by a bold leap from his window, whence the name by which he is known in the legendary history of his race. Then came Ludwig the Iron, around whom strange stories cluster; then Ludwig the gentle; afterwards another Ludwig, with "a winning tongue, sweet address, and noble manners." The chief story of peace connected with the weather-beaten feudal walls is that there was a great deal of musical skill here in the year 1207 when Minnesängers assembled in the large Sängersaal, and filled it with their songs and melodies.

The castle has been restored within the last twenty years, and between visits I paid in 1856 and 1874 very great changes had taken place in the edifice. Now the restoration of the galleries, halls, and chambers is complete, and all is done which skilled art and liberal wealth are able to accomplish. The beauty of the situation, the picturesqueness of the castle, the historical associations, and the arrangements made for the entertainment of visitors, have rendered the Wartburg one of the most attractive spots in Germany. When one of the official guides was asked by the correspondent of the "Daily News" (1874) how many people visited it yearly, "Sixty thousand," he answered, "and the place had been rented for some years past, first at seven hundred thalers; for the year about closing, two thousand; and in future four thousand thalers. The old lady who has been running the establishment has become rich, and intends to retire now altogether from business. Since the charge per head for viewing the Wartburg is five silver groschen, and sixty thousand persons visit the place annually, the gross income of the proprietress must be ten thousand thalers yearly, beside the profits of the hotel and restauration."

It is beyond my province to describe the contents of this interesting edifice; our business is simply with what relates to Martin Luther.

From May, 1521, to March, 1522, he remained in kind and hospitable durance, under the protection of his fast friend, the

Elector Frederick of Saxony. The table of the prisoner was supplied with Rhenish wine and plenty of game; his acquaintances were allowed to visit him; they came at night, and in the morning assembled in the castle hall to hear from his lips the doctrines of the Reformation. There was a great air of mystery, for obvious reasons, at first thrown around his concealment, and therefore he did not write to any one for some days: when he recommenced correspondence he dated his letters from "The Regions of the Air," "The Regions of the Birds," "My Hermitage," "The Isle of Patmos." That fountain of poetry which lay hid in Luther's robust and vigorous nature bubbles up beautifully in such expressions; and refreshing must have been the views caught by him the morning after he first slept in the Wartburg, and opened his window on the breadths of hill and woodland spreading out before his eyes in the fresh green robes and the pure white blossoms of early May. What he thought of the legends of Elizabeth, clustering as flowers about the courtyard, corridors, and chambers of the castle, we do not know. He must have been familiar with them in his boyhood. At all events, with an eye open to the loveliness of nature, he had, with all his hatred of superstition, an eye for the moral in old church myths, since in his "Table Talk" he speaks of St. Christopher and the child Jesus, remarking, "'Tis a fine Christian poem; and so is the legend of St. George. George, in the Greek, means a builder that builds edifices justly and with regularity, and who resists and drives away the enemies that would assault and damage them." Though Luther's Greek is here at fault—for Georgios signifies a husbandman, not a builder—he indicates an appreciation of the significance of a mythical story; therefore it is not unlikely that he turned to good practical account traditions about the saintly Landgravine, such as passed the lips of the castle household and the peasantry scattered around its rocky base.

There are two parts of the Wartburg closely identified with the

CHAPEL IN THE WARTBURG.

Reformer's residence there. The first is the chapel, constructed in the main building. It has a vaulted roof with heavy Romanesque columns, its sombre appearance being relieved by the painting and gilding it underwent in the recent restoration. Some wall paintings were at the time brought to light, from which the old whitewash has been removed, and the Virgin Mary, the Apostles Peter and Paul, and certain emblematical figures reappear in their original colours. The stained windows are brilliant, and the emblematical pillar sculpturing is very curious. Here the Reformer conducted religious worship. The altar at which he ministered and the pulpit from which he preached still remain; but beyond these and the general outline of the chapel, its aspect at present must be considerably different from what it was in his time, for alterations were made in this portion of the castle by the Grand Duke Ernst in 1625.

The second and far more important part connected with Luther is the Ritterhaus, in which he was lodged. It stands on the right-hand side of the courtyard as you pass through the gateway, and it continues unaltered. The little flight of steps—the narrow door—the old device of Samson slaying the lion—the stone table in the hall, remain as they were the midnight of the 4th of May, 1521, when the armed men hurried their willing captive over the drawbridge and through the low archway of the fortress. This hall is on the ground floor; ascending a staircase, we reach the room which Luther occupied as his chamber and study. It is rather a small room, now wainscotted for the most part, with a portion of the original wall in plaster. Near this part stands a Dutch stove, dug out of the castle rubbish, and a bedstead in which Luther is said to have slept in the castle of Gleichen. The table at which he wrote has been carried away in chips, but in its place is found another at which we are told he sat as a boy in his father's house. Over it is his portrait by Cranach the elder, with portraits of his parents by Cranach the younger.

A framed autograph letter by Luther hangs on the wall; under it are his father's mining lamp and the money-box which the Eisenach schoolboy carried about on his begging excursions. A joint of a whale's backbone, used as his footstool, lies on the floor, and a piece of the beech at Altenstein where he was captured is also preserved. Chests, with Bibles of Luther's translation, and other books, complete the furniture of this interesting room, where, in the guise of a squire, with his hair and beard grown very long, and attended by "two noble youths," he spent so many months.

On the plastered portion of the wall is shown the spot where he threw the inkstand at the devil.

A sceptical generation, repulsed by any allusion to what is supernatural, discredits the story, as if its truth depended on an actual Satanic appearance.

Luther constantly talked and wrote about the devil. "I hold," he says, at a later date, after the rebellion of Münzer, the controversy with Carlstadt, and the disputes with the Zwinglians, "that I alone have stood in twenty tempests and commotions of the devil. First, there were the Papists; yea, I think all the world should clearly know how many hurricanes, bulls, and books the devil through them has thrown at me; how he has torn me to pieces, and brought me to nought. I, indeed, have sometimes a little stirred up the Papists, and yet effected nothing by it, except that they have increased their wrath and fury to this day without ceasing. Just as I was almost dying from fear of this raging of the devil, he breaks through another hole, even Münzer and his insurrection, in order to blow out my candle altogether. As Christ stops up this opening, the devil drives in some panes of my window, by means of Carlstadt, and so roars and howls that I thought he would carry away light, wax, and wick together. But God preserved the taper from being quenched. Then came the Sacramentalists, and the Anabaptists, and drove in both doors and windows, endeavouring to extinguish the light entirely.

LUTHER'S STUDY IN THE WARTBURG.

They did their best, but they did not accomplish their wish."[1] The "Table Talk" abounds in references to Satan and his temptations.

When we think of the order of Luther's mind; of his vivid imagination, of his strained nervous system when engaged in study, of the objective form into which he cast his thoughts, and of his habitual reference to the spirit of darkness as busy in the world every moment, it is by no means unlikely that in some fit of abstraction, when wrestling with a difficulty in his work, he should give what Coleridge calls *outness* to his own ideas, and, in a fit of spiritual frenzy, take up his inkstand and fling it at what—for the instant—appeared to him a palpable foe. Men of genius create forms which haunt them as realities, and I have little doubt that the far-famed tale of the Wartburg had a foundation in fact; and assuredly it is a mythical representation of his great life work, namely, by means of books flinging ink at Satan, and something more. Other circumstances connected with his abode at the Wartburg might have something to do with such an hallucination. He suffered from ill-health through sedentary employment, and the suspension, at times, of active habits. He passed sleepless nights, experienced bodily anguish, and uttered cries like "those of a woman in her travail,"—these are his words. It may have been whilst under the effects of such maladies he had dark visions of "the prince of the power of the air;" and, in addition, the castle at the time was disturbed by strange noises; as if a hundred hogsheads had been tumbled from the top to the bottom of the staircase. So much was the Reformer troubled with these disturbances—which Michelet attributes partly to tricks played by members of the household—that he was glad to change his sleeping-chamber. These circumstances would lead to the idea of the place being haunted; and such an idea, not uncommonly entertained by the wisest of that age, might influence Luther in his visions.

[1] This was written not long before his death.

At all events, Luther, in that room, did throw plenty of ink at the devil; for there he wrote against auricular confession, the abuse of the mass, and clerical and monastic vows; there, also, he composed expositions of certain psalms, finished his Declaration of the Magnificat, began to write his Church Homilies, and worked hard upon his translation of the New Testament.

Here he began his great work as a translator, but here he did not finish it; and therefore what I have to say upon this important subject shall be deferred to the chapter on Wittenberg, where the whole translation was published in 1534.

The period of Luther's residence in the Wartburg is peculiarly rich in illustrative correspondence, and from many pages of his letters may be culled passages bearing on his habits and experience. As Coleridge says in "The Friend," there can scarcely be conceived a more delightful volume than might be made from De Wette's edition of Luther's Letters, "if they were translated in the simple, sinewy, idiomatic, hearty mother tongue of the original." . The first letter dated from the Wartburg was written on the 12th of May. "What are you doing?" he asks Philip Melancthon; "are you not praying that my retirement may promote the glory of God? I fear I shall be thought a deserter from the battle-field, but I could not resist those who counselled me in this course. Here I sit all day thinking of God's Church; the Roman Antichrist is a horrible proof of God's anger. I abhor my hardness of heart that I am not melted into tears. God have mercy on us. Be thou instant as a minister of the word; thou knowest thy calling and gifts. Thus far I have stood in the front of the battle. Next they will seek thy life."

On the 10th of June he describes himself at the same time as most idle and most busy, adding, "I learn and write Hebrew and Greek without intermission," thus indicating the preparation he was making for his momentous life task. It is curious to find that then, and even later, the place of his abode was little known, and that the clouds of mystery in which the Elector had shrouded him only gradually dispersed. On the 15th of July he informs Spalatin that Duke George had only just heard the rumour that he was at the Wartburg.

It is not generally noticed that towards the close of the year he left his place of concealment and returned for a short visit to Wittenberg; yet such is the fact, as appears from a letter written in November to Spalatin, at the house of Amsdorf, in which he speaks of his renewing sweet intercourse with old friends.

From accounts of his life at the Wartburg we learn how fond he was of rambling beyond the castle gate, and picking wild berries; how he went out hunting as "Junker Georg," and found a hare caught in a trap, which he wrapped in his garment and meant to save, but the dogs got hold of it and killed it, as the devil and the Pope do the souls of men; how he rode in disguise to Gotha, Erfurt, Reinhardsbrunn, and Marksuhl, and how, at one of these places, he was recognised by the inhabitants, and had to make off as quickly as possible.

As I think of beautiful drives in the Thüringerwald, in the direction of these towns,—now climbing pine-clad hills, now winding down into grassy dells, and now passing rocks of red and purple hue, I can imagine him in some pathless quarter of the forest, at the tail of the hounds, rushing in at the death of a buck or a boar, amidst the cries of the Herzog's huntsmen. As I think of beautiful walks along the Marienthal and the Annathal—two fascinating valleys, especially the last, where you stroll for a long distance through a narrow defile of moss-covered rocks, so close together on the two sides that one person can scarcely pass another, —overhead leafy arches, and underfoot a wooden pathway covering a brook, where waters may be heard gurgling beneath, I picture Luther plunging into depths of verdure, and finding in trees and wild flowers, hares and birds, images of spiritual truths, and sources of playful thought.

I am aware that the present path through the Annathal was not made until 1833 ; I only mean that such parts of this charming neighbourhood as were accessible in the sixteenth century, Martin Luther would be likely to explore.

A great change went on in his views during these months of confinement. He saw more and more into the depths of Popery, and the evils of monasticism. Indeed, it may be said that it was in the Wartburg that he altogether ceased to be a monk, and prepared conscientiously for his own pure-minded marriage, and for laying fresh corner-stones on which to build up the domestic life of Germany.

But the studies and discipline of the old castle were interrupted by news from Wittenberg. He considered the cause of the Reformation to be imperilled by what was going on there, and he began to exclaim, " Oh that I were at Wittenberg ! " Thought and action were closely connected in the Reformer's nature, and he determined, at all hazards, to return to the scene of his former labours. The death of Leo X. in the month of December, 1521, and the election of Adrian VI., who adopted a different line of policy from his predecessor, made a considerable difference in Luther's position, and left him little or no reason to be anxious about his personal security. In 1522 he started from his retreat ; and on his way home stopped at Jena, where occurred what is related in the following characteristic anecdote, which we owe to Kessler of St. Gall, one of the persons included in the scene described :

"At the gate of the city we met a respectable-looking man, who accosted us in a friendly manner, and asked whither we were going so late, . . . and whether we had inquired for entertainment at the 'Black Bear.' . . . He pointed it out to us at a little distance from the city. . . . The innkeeper met us at the door, and led us into a room. Here we found a man, sitting alone at a table, with a small book before him, who greeted us kindly, and invited us to take a seat beside him. . . . We took him to

THE WARTBURG.

be a knight, as he wore, according to the custom of the country, a red cap, small-clothes, and a doublet, and had a sword at his side, on which he leaned, resting on the hilt. He asked whence we were; but immediately added, 'You are Swiss: from what part of Switzerland?' We replied, 'St. Gall.' He then inquired, 'If, as I suppose, you are on your way to Wittenberg, you will find there good countrymen of yours, namely, Jerome Schurff and his brother Augustine.' 'To which we replied, 'We have letters to them.' We now asked if he could give us any information about Martin Luther; whether he was at Wittenberg, or elsewhere. He answered, 'I have certain knowledge that he is not at Wittenberg now, but he will be soon. Philip Melancthon, however, is there as teacher of Greek, with others who teach Hebrew.'

"'Sir,' said he, 'what do men in Switzerland think of Luther?' We replied, 'Variously, as everywhere else. Some cannot sufficiently bless and praise God for having, through this man, made known His truth and exposed error; others condemn him as an intolerable heretic!' 'Especially the clergy,' interrupted he. By this conversation we were made to feel ourselves quite at home with the stranger, and one of us took the book which lay before him, and found it was a Hebrew Psalter. This increased our curiosity to know who he was. As the day declined, and it grew dark, our host, aware of our longing, came to the table and said, 'Friends, had you been here two days ago, you could have had your desire, for Luther sat here at this table.' We were provoked that we were too late, and began to abuse the bad roads which had detained us on our journey. After a little while the host called me to the door, and said, 'Since you manifest so earnest a desire to see Luther, you should know that it is he who sat by you.'"

The travellers afterwards visited Wittenberg, and were kindly received by the Reformer.[1]

[1] I have condensed the story related by Kessler, and elaborated by Merle d'Aubigné, book ix., c. viii.

XII.

SWABIA AND THE BAVARIAN HIGHLANDS.

"WERE I to travel much," says Luther, "I would go nowhere of a readier will, than into Swabia and Bavaria." Through these countries he passed on his way from Wittenberg to Rome—in 1510 according to the Heidelberg Chronicle, in 1511 according to Melancthon.

Swabia is a very indefinite landmark to guide us in quest of the Reformer's footprints. The name denoted one of the states included within what Mr. Freeman, in his "Historical Geography of Europe," calls the kingdom of Germany, broken up before the close of the Middle Ages. "No part of Germany was more cut up into small states than the old land of the Hohenstaufen. A crowd of principalities, secular and ecclesiastical, among them the lesser principalities of the Hohenzollern House of free cities, and of outlying possessions of the House of Austria made up the main part of the [Swabian] circle. Strasburg, Augsburg, Constanz, St. Gallen, Chur, Zurich, are among the great bishoprics and the other ecclesiastical foundations of the old Swabia." The name had changed its meaning somewhat in Luther's time, and did not include so wide a territory as it had done before; probably he intended by it a region extending from Augsburg, on the north-east, to somewhere about the lake of Constance, to the south-west. He travelled through Heidelberg, as we have seen; and then proceeding south-east, entered Swabia, but what was his exact route, and what places he stopped at we do not know. Tradition says he went to Munich, but that lies outside the Swabian circle as just defined. At any rate, he penetrated into Bavaria, after crossing Swabia, and he mentions distinctly Füssen in Bavaria, as one of the places he went through on his way to Italy.

Füssen is worthy of special notice. It is a characteristic Bavarian country town, and is romantically situated at the foot of the Highlands, which form the boundaries of Switzerland and the Tyrol. It is a gateway into some of the most charming Alpine scenery of Europe.

Two summers ago[1] I approached it from Kempten, on the Ulm and Lindau Railway. A carriage-drive takes you in a few hours to Nesselwang, along a road which leads to a mountain range amidst which are embedded numerous bewitching valleys, lakes and villages. Nesselwang is a typical sort of place, with a good long picturesque street; houses and shutters are painted in different colours, the eaves project over the thoroughfare, where people pack up their winter wood, and women sit out of doors on benches, to gossip and to work. The church has in it several frescoes; also skeletons of two saints attired in tinsel and jewellery; and the ends of the aisle benches have on them burnt-in marks and greasy blotched mementoes of candles fixed there on festival occasions. In the portico of the edifice is a rude model of Gethsemane, below which, placed in niches, are eleven skulls. All this takes us back to Luther's time, and gives an idea of objects with which his journey towards Italy made him familiar. Indeed he had seen plenty of churches in his own country decked after this fashion.

[1] 1881.

Füssen is a town of between one and two thousand inhabitants, and is jammed into a narrow defile, through which the waters of the Lech rush from its source on the hills, down towards the Bavarian plains. The gorge takes the name of Füssen, so it is said, from its ancient appellation of Fauces Julia. The Bishops of Augsburg had a castle on the rocky heights above the town, and the street with the castle over it presents a picturesque view to the traveller as he drives down to the little inn of the Post. An abbey of St. Magnus was connected with Füssen, but the existing church of the sequestrated foundation had not been built when Luther visited the spot.

Five miles from Füssen stands the castle of Hohenschwangen, where Luther was entertained, it is said, during the Augsburg Diet of 1530. Whether it was just then, or at some other time, it seems probable from the idea which lingers over the spot, that the Reformer really was sheltered within the hospitable walls of this old fortress,—which passed from the Guelph family to the Emperor Frederic Barbarossa. Conradin of Swabia has also left his name on the time-stained edifice,—now restored by the King of Bavaria, who loves the neighbourhood, and sometimes visits it; when my family and I were there, he was engaged building a new castle opposite the old one. The old castle occupies a wooded eminence, and in the halls and apartments are seen Munich pictures, stained glass, statuary, armour, and other adornments. Visitors over and over again meet with something or other relative to the legendary Schwan-ritter, or Knight of the Swan, from whose adventures the place takes its name. The figure of a swan is everywhere, and the terrace, enlivened by three fountains, looks down on the lake of the Swan. As we passed from one part to another, now in Bertha's chamber, then in the hero's hall, plenty of artistic objects arrested attention, till the whole culminated in Luther's room, where we were assured that the Reformer tarried when the Diet of Augsburg was being held.

The tradition has certainly indented itself deeply on the castle of Hohenschwangen.

Luther speaks of the country people in Swabia and Bavaria as "kind-hearted and hospitable, and forward to treat strangers and pilgrims charitably, and give them full their money's worth." When he said this, it was in reference to his journey through the region Romewards; and it indicates that he found the rustic hostleries comfortable and cheap. They are so still, and I have pleasant remembrances of entertainment under long roofs, half barn and half habitation, where the Bavarian farmer, without professing to be an innkeeper will receive the tourist as a guest, giving him a hearty welcome and fair entertainment. I recollect, too, that at nightfall the farm servants came into the kitchen to chant a litany before going to bed. I wonder whether family worship was so maintained when Luther was in Bavaria!

XIII.

LUTHER'S JOURNEYS DURING THE PEASANTS' WAR.

THE principal travellers in the sixteenth century were princes, soldiers, merchants, and ecclesiastics; amongst the latter, few, as to the extent and the number of journeys, equalled Luther. None others left such a mark on the places visited.

Out of travels in Saxony and the neighbourhood an interesting group may be arranged round incidents of an untoward character, which occurred in connection with early Protestantism. Two deep streams of social excitement appeared, greatly troubling the Reformers, and affording to their enemies a malicious satisfaction.

One was religious. Everybody must see that an outbreak such as overthrew the Mediæval Church necessarily involved wild sentiment and fanatical conduct. Accordingly, we do not go far with the story of Lutheranism before our attention is arrested by lawless proceedings. Though Carlstadt, who took a conspicuous part at Leipzig, has suffered from the misrepresentations of adversaries, there can be no doubt that he adopted very rash and mischievous opinions, and rushed into revolutionary excesses, which could not but cover him with disgrace. But Thomas Münzer affords a much more revolting example of wild and revolutionary conduct ; beginning his career simply as an advocate of visionary spiritualism, and as a pretender to supernatural gifts, he ended by taking the lead in a rebellious war, for which he paid the penalty of his life.

The excitement with which these men are identified, created in Luther the most distressing anxiety. With both these persons he came into contact ; and their movements occasioned a memorable journey in the year 1522, which it is worth while to follow.

Zwickau is a picturesque town on the banks of the Zwickauer-Mulde, in the kingdom of Saxony, and is connected with the Leipzig and Hof Railway by a branch line. The district around is rich in coal beds, and not very far off are extensive cobalt mines and smalt works, together with fields of porcelain earth, so that the town abounds in manufactures, and carries on a prosperous trade. It contains five churches, one of which, St. Mary's, is a fine Gothic edifice, with a grandly carved altar-piece of life-sized figures, executed in 1479. Another elaborate work of art in the sacristy, representing the Holy Sepulchre, and a baptismal chapel adorned by a picture of one of the Cranachs, take us back to the days of the Reformation. Luther seems to have been familiar with the place, and to have been fond of ascending the tall tower, "on account of the pleasing view it commands ;" but what brings the town under our notice now is the visit which he paid to it in the month of April, 1522. It was at that time in a state of great excitement. Nicholas Storch had selected twelve followers, whom he called apostles, one of whom was Thomas Münzer. Being gifted with a rude and fiery eloquence, the latter roused attention to the doctrines which he and his associates had espoused, and made a number of converts. These Zwickau prophets, as they were designated, aroused the indignation of Luther; and in a letter addressed to Spalatin, the 12th of April, he refers to them in his characteristic style as "instruments of Satan, full of a proud and vehement spirit, and deaf to the voice of reason." On the 21st he appears to have had an interview with Carlstadt, in which he deprecated the thought of controversy, and exhorted him to quietude and peace; but before the end of the month we find him on the road to Zwickau, travelling in a car and dressed as a layman, to escape the notice of the Saxon authorities, for "had he fallen into the hands of the angry duke, it might probably have been all over with him."[1]

He preached in the town, and people flocked from neighbouring places to the number of fourteen thousand. St. Mary's Church could not receive the multitudes—and to have preached from the tall tower he was so fond of, certainly would not have been convenient,—therefore he ascended the balcony of the Rathhaus, and there addressed the crowd in the square—a crowd reckoned at twenty-five thousand. As he spoke with warmth an old woman was seen with a haggard eye, "stretching out her lean arms, and looking as if with her bony hand she would keep back the crowd as it was pressing to the feet of Jesus Christ. Her wild screams interrupted the preacher." Seckendorf declares it was the devil, who, assuming the form of an old woman, wanted to excite a tumult. "But it was in vain; the preacher's words silenced the evil spirit; enthusiasm took possession of the thousands of listeners; people shook hands in token of mutual concord; and ere long the monks, confounded and unable to compose the storm, saw themselves obliged to leave Zwickau." At all events, Luther was equal to the occasion, and made a wonderful impression on his audience.

On his way to Zwickau he stopped at a place called Boma and at Altenburg—the latter a well-known station on the Leipzig Railway, where there is a *schloss* on the escarped rock, a residence of the Emperor Charlemagne, still rich in ancient armour. Altenburg seems to have interested Luther a good deal, and for its

[1] D'Aubigné, vol. ii., p. 250.

LUTHER PREACHING TO THE PEASANTS.

religious welfare he felt deeply solicitous, as appears not only from his preaching, but from letters he wrote to the burgomaster and pastor of the town, on his return home. The people of the duchy are Wends by descent—a Sclavonic race, preserving an odd female costume, which consists of a Highland petticoat with a wicker-work corset, the head-gear being "a conical cap of portentous dimensions." As this probably was the dress worn by a good many of Luther's hearers, his congregation must have exhibited an odd sight as they gathered together.

Another stream of religious fanaticism broke forth in the autumn of the same year at Erfurt. The Reformation laid hold on the clergy of Luther's former residence, and to a large extent on the students of Luther's university. The canons of the place having expelled one of their body for adopting the Lutheran faith, the students became incensed, and made a violent attack on the old forms of worship and on the houses of those who persevered in it. Münzer and Carlstadt could not tolerate the use of images, the celebration of mass, the invocation of saints, and other parts of the Roman Catholic ritual, and therefore encouraged iconoclasm and similar acts of violence. This spirit of destruction moved some of the Erfurt Reformers ; and it seemed likely to produce excesses beyond what had been at first committed. Hence Luther determined to visit Erfurt, and use his influence to stay the rising storm.

This journey he took in the month of October, and on his way he tarried and preached at Weimar—probably in the Schloss Kirche, or Church of St. James, where his friend Lucas Cranach was afterwards buried. His entrance into Erfurt would have been an ovation if he would have permitted it ; for he was exceedingly popular there, and crowds waited at the gates to give him welcome. But he slid quietly in, though he could not avoid being lionized in the evening, at one of the parsonages. He preached three times on the two following days, and then went back to Weimar, where he remained some little time, addressing eager audiences again and again. Luther's oratory was in great request—like that of popular preachers in the present day; and letters and deputations of all sorts came to his house at Wittenberg, from places obscure as well as from places distinguished. Just before starting on the Weimar and Erfurt expedition, he said at the end of a letter to Spalatin, " I am off to Leyswick," wherever that might be, " having been oft invited and urged to go."

We must now notice the political excitement which at this time rushed through Germany. It is a great mistake to suppose that what are commonly called the Peasant Wars originated with the Reformation. They arose out of the feudal system. Oppressive laws crushed the lower classes; irresponsible power lodged in the lords of the soil produced intense suffering; consequently those who were the victims of manifold wrongs at last turned against their masters and endeavoured to shake off the galling yoke of iron. Of those who trampled upon their inferiors, the spiritual lords, according to all accounts, were the worst. Bishops and abbots figure with a pre-eminently cruel aspect in the chronicles of the period. We read of a revolt against the Abbot of Kemplen in 1491, and of a rebellion in the Bishopric of Spires in 1503. There were risings at different periods against Dukes and Counts, who thought more of their own interests than the welfare of their subjects.

But the years 1524 and 1525 witnessed the more revolutionary outbreaks on the part of the German peasantry; and it is remarkable how purely secular were the causes assigned for opposition to the established authorities. In one case the peasants complained "that they were obliged to hunt for snails, wind yarn, gather strawberries, cherries, and sloes, and do other such like things; they had to work for their lords and ladies in fine weather, and for themselves in the rain. Huntsmen and hounds ran about without considering the damage they did." One smiles at the trivial nature of such details, yet they indicate how the peasants were treated as serfs, whilst they clearly prove that civil and political, not religious, grievances lay at the root of the disaffection in rural districts. The religious element, however, soon mingled with what was secular.

"The political excitement," says Ranke, "was not produced by the preaching, but the religious enthusiasts caught the political fever." Even Thomas Münzer did not begin as a political agitator, but, after playing the part of a frenzied fanatic, was drawn into the vortex of rebellion and carried away by the torrent. Carlstadt throughout was more of a religious enthusiast than anything else. Entangled in these complications, Suabian, Franconian, Thuringian, and Saxon peasants appear as rebels in the latter half of 1524. The tide of revolution surged up to Luther's door, and he could not rest. In August he left Wittenberg to see what he could do to stem the angry waters. He appears at Weimar on the 14th, where he wrote a letter to the Senate of Mühlhausen warning them against Münzer. Next we find a letter dated the 21st, addressed to the Princes Frederick and John on the same absorbing subject; and an exhortation by Luther is preserved, addressed to all Christians, warning them against the sin of rebellion, and entreating them to confine themselves to moral means for the overthrow of Popery and other evils.

At Jena on the 22nd he is found preaching with great vehemence, directing his denunciations against "two sorts of fanaticism, that of the seditious enthusiasts who were now beginning to disturb the peace of Germany, and that of the image-breakers." Carlstadt was present, and felt highly incensed at the preacher's tone. Calling on him at his inn, the "Black Bear," he held a conference with Luther in the presence of witnesses. Carlstadt indignantly denied that he had any share in the rebellion, and Luther admitted his denial; yet immediately they entered upon an altercation as to the doctrine of the Lord's Supper, Luther throwing down on the table a dollar as the pledge of battle, and Carlstadt accepting it. Presently we learn that they shook hands and drank each other's health. Again collisions were renewed; but Luther, as was the wont of his generous nature, after loading him with reproaches, engaged in kindly offices on his behalf.

Carlstadt had established a printing-press at Jena, where, at that time, there was no university, and he lived not far off, at Orlamünde, on the River Saale, where he was very popular.

Luther, in spite of warnings to the contrary, proceeded to that place, and met with a reception unlike what he enjoyed in most towns which had adopted the doctrines of the Reformation. According to all historians, he had a narrow escape. He says himself, "I had good reason to rejoice that I fortunately slipped away from among them with my life, and was not overwhelmed with stones and dirt. Some of them, as I was retiring, uttered the most horrid imprecations against me, and prayed God that I might break my neck before I got away from the town."[1]

In the winter of 1524-5 a manifesto of grievances suffered by the peasants made its appearance, couched in moderate terms, and breathing a reasonable spirit. It commenced by referring to the charge of disobedience and rebellion brought against them: and then after repelling the charge proceeded to state complaints and to supplicate redress. It is curious that the only article of a religious character is the first, in which they demanded the right of choosing their own pastors. They next declared their willingness to pay the great tithes, but they resisted the payment of small ones. This was followed by a protest against being treated as serfs; by a petition for the privilege of gathering wood in the forests, and the diminution of feudal service and payments; and by complaints of high rents, of the partial administration of justice, and of the enclosure of commons. In conclusion, they appealed to

---

[1] Quoted by Waddington, "Hist. of Reformation." See also Ranke's "History of the Reformation," vol. ii., p. 88.

Scripture. If the temper manifested in this document had been general, and if it had been met in a conciliatory manner, matters might have been amicably arranged ; but the majority of the discontented must have cherished feelings very different from those so temperately expressed, and, on the other hand, it is certain the German lords were more disposed to crush than to soothe their irritated dependants.

The violent spirits carried the day. Revolt spread like wildfire, and Thomas Münzer from a preacher became a warrior, unfurled the flag of defiance at Mühlhausen, and resolved, at all hazards, to carry his cause into the field. In other neighbourhoods, many of the peasants took up arms, and civil war flashed as lightning in every direction.

Luther watched the storm ; and in a letter to Amsdorf, the 11th of April, after referring to Carlstadt's proceedings, remarked : " Münzer is King and Emperor at Mühlhausen, and not merely Doctor." Mühlhausen lies to the north of Eisenach and Erfurt, on the road to the Harz country, with a noble Gothic church of the fourteenth century. It is a walled town, pleasantly situated on the banks of the River Unstrut; now it is a part of the Prussian dominions, but at the time of the Reformation it was a free city of the empire. Being occupied by Münzer and his misguided supporters, it became the centre of the revolt, the citadel of the rustic rebellion. Into the heart of this disturbed district, a region he had been familiar with from his youth, Luther determined to penetrate, and therefore set out on another of the journeys now under review.

He started from Wittenberg on Easter Sunday, April the 16th, immediately after his sermon, much to the surprise of Melancthon, and travelled at once to Seeburg (*Lake Town*), a small village lying between the Mansfeld Lakes,[1] not far from Halle, and in the midst of a mining district where the insurgent spirit was rife.

[1] See page 5.

From Seeburg he proceeded to Stolberg, the birthplace of Münzer, on the borders of the Harz country, with a castle romantically situated on the neighbouring heights. Stolberg is not far from Nördhausen, a curious old place, planted near the Golden Mead, in the midst of a rich corn country, boasting still of an enormous figure in stone, symbolical of town rights, and also of a picture in the church of the funeral at Nain, in which the artist, Lucas Cranach, has introduced Luther and Melancthon as mourners.

From Nördhausen to Erfurt there runs a railway which brings the traveller from the former to the latter place in three hours. Very much longer would be the time required to cross the distance in Luther's day. After performing that journey he proceeded from Erfurt to Weimar and Orlamünde. Orlamünde is fifteen miles from Weimar, and near to Jena, as we have seen. Luther visited Orlamünde and Jena on this occasion, and also another town, which Seckendorf calls Calac. This, no doubt, is a Latinized name for *Kahla*, which is situated in the valley of the Saale, on the high road between Orlamünde and Jena. Stierler's Atlas shows the distance from Jena as about three English miles. Blackie, in his "Imperial Gazetteer," describes it as containing 2,463 inhabitants, surrounded by walls, having three gates, and three suburbs, two churches, and an hospital, also manufactories, tan-yards and dyeing works. On the opposite side of the river is the old castle of Leuchtenburg; and on a hill overhanging the public road the ruined castle of Orlamünde. Through this little cluster of towns Luther worked his way when the peasants agitated the public mind. In the churches he preached, in the houses he talked, and by all possible means sought to subdue the commotion.

Such is the itinerary of the Reformer on this expedition, as indicated by Seckendorf;[1] and though we have no details

---

[1] "Com. de Luther, tome ii." p. 9.

preserved, we are enabled to form some idea of its inconveniences, from a record, by a far different traveller, Lorenzo Orio, the Venetian ambassador, who was at the same time passing through another district disturbed by the war. He writes, on the 2nd of May, that since his last letter from Augsburg, he has been "in great trouble and peril, in a besieged city, and compelled to perform very rough journeys over mountains and by unusual passes, dodging in a thousand ways, to avoid the rabid and sanguinary peasants, who have placed all Germany in tumult and confusion." "The reason is," he remarks, "that all are in arms; in the villages and territories there remain but lads and women; and the cities have been abandoned by the greater part of the artizans to follow the armies. For not only have the peasants risen against their masters, the lords and grandees, but the townspeople have rebelled against the clergy, and compelled them to be content with so much of their revenues as may suffice for food and raiment, leaving the rest at the disposal of the city for expenditure on the common need for the general and public benefit. Should this excitement continue the whole world will be thrown into confusion." [1]

On the 3rd of May Luther was at Weimar, as we find from his correspondence, for on that day he wrote to Frederick Myconius at Gotha, quoting the beautiful words, so comforting amidst confusion and sorrow, "In the world ye shall have tribulation; but be of good cheer, I have overcome the world." On the 4th we find him at Seeburg again, whither he must have travelled with haste. Seckendorf, after enumerating the places visited, says Luther had intended to travel farther, but was prevented by the death of the Elector Frederick. The Elector died in May. On the 5th of May, according to the date given in Luther's Letters, the Reformer was

[1] May 2, 1525. Lorenzo Orio, Venetian ambassador, on his way to England. Brown's "Calendar of Venetian State Papers," vol. iii., p. 430.

at home in Wittenberg. Probably the illness of the Elector hastened his journey; and on his return he edited and issued his famous reply to the peasants' manifesto.

First addressing himself to the princes and nobles, he told them that the peasantry had drawn up twelve articles, containing demands so obviously equitable, that the mere circumstance of their being made, "dishonoured their superiors before God and man, and realised the 107th Psalm, which poureth contempt on princes." He then addressed the peasants, exhorting them to moderation and justice, warning them against demagogues, and distinguishing between the good and the bad who had taken part in the movement. He held up himself to them as an example, declaring he had never drawn the sword—never attempted to revolt, but had always inculcated passive obedience; a course of conduct which had not only preserved his life, but had advanced religion. He then examined in detail the twelve articles, and took exception to the way in which some of them were expressed.

Though not until after Luther had completed his journey did he issue this publication,[1] it appears he had not at the time become aware of the atrocities committed by Münzer and his adherents; and this accounts for the mildness of the Reformer's rebuke of the peasants. Indeed, it indicates that at the moment of writing he only apprehended the possibility of war; it is clear he could not have felt it was waging round him; hence I infer it must have been composed some time before it was printed. However that may be, the publication came too late to produce any effect, and it is uncertain what good it could have accomplished had it appeared earlier; this, however, is probable, that in the address we have the arguments and sentiments of Luther at the time of his journey to Seeburg and the other places just mentioned; and therefore it may be taken as a mirror, reflecting the substance of

[1] I have seen an original printed copy. It has no date; but Seckendorf enables us to determine that point approximately. "Com. de Luther," tome ii. pp. 9 and 7.

his sermons in one church pulpit after another throughout the troubled district.

Münzer's proclamation, dated Mühlhausen, 1525,"—which most likely fell into Luther's hands after he had sent forth his reply to the peasants—breathed threatenings and slaughter to a terrific degree, crying, "On, on ! while the fire is burning, and the sword is reeking ; let not the one be quenched or the other sheathed."

The madness of Münzer and his party brought matters to a crisis ; and on the 15th of May the decisive battle of Frankenhausen was fought, and Münzer was taken prisoner and executed. By the middle of June the insurgent flames were extinguished in streams of blood. The conquerors were in many cases as merciless as the vanquished had been defiant. It is sad to notice that Luther, in a tract written after his reply to the peasants, pours forth his indignation against the rebels with unbridled violence, and in a public defence, as well as in private letters, expresses himself in a manner utterly inconsistent with the spirit of the gospel.

Yet though in this, and some other epochs of his life, he manifested an unjustifiable temper, it ought to be noticed that he never appears as a political agitator. We do not find him interfering with State affairs, plunging into local questions of a simply secular kind, or seeking to revolutionize the forms of temporal government. He took up the controversy in the peasants' war entirely in its moral and religious aspects. He contended for freedom from Popish tyranny, but he was a staunch friend of social order. He reproved the peasants as pursuing a course which was anti-Christian, and irreconcilable with justice, benevolence, and common humanity. His mission was of a spiritual order, and he always acted under the conviction that he was a minister of God, the righteous Judge.

XIV.

MARBURG, ON THE LAHN.

A VISIT to Marburg, in search of Luther's haunts, brings us once more across the path of Elizabeth of Hungary—there it is her short life-story terminates, and there she sleeps in the church which bears her name. Those who have travelled on the line between Cassel and Frankfort will remember catching sight of three spires, on slightly-rising ground, near the Marburg Station, with the town and castle rising beyond it. Such as have stopped and explored the place can never forget the specimen of pointed Gothic to which those spires belong. It pertains to the period of transition from the German Romanesque (1235 to 1283), and was the fruit of a vow made by Elizabeth, as Landgravine of Hesse. It contains the shrine which enclosed her body, a structure of curious workmanship, now stripped of the costly gems it once displayed. The shrine was as popular with pilgrims in Germany as Becket's was in England: for in this case, as in that, the steps above which it stood are worn away by the knees of worshippers.

The statuette of Elizabeth in the choir is an exquisite production.

VIEW OF MARBURG.

Her crowned forehead has a bandage over the brows, and she holds in her hand a model of the church : a grotesque figure kneels at her feet—a beggar, we presume ; art generally representing her as attended by some one in that character. The figures are painted ; and, it may be added, the stained glass in the choir is very beautiful.

The town of Marburg wrought a spell on my own imagination and that of my daughter the evening we arrived ; and, attracted by the moonlight throwing out in dark relief the castle of the Landgraves, I left our hotel, and climbed a steep street, bordered by twisted acacia trees, till I reached the centre of the town ; the domestic architecture, as far as the shadows permitted examination, giving promise, all the way, of an archæological treat the next morning. The next morning this promise was fulfilled ; for a more thoroughly old-fashioned town—one more free from modern innovations—one carrying the mind more completely back to the Middle Ages, I do not know ; nor am I aware of any part of Germany where the antique costume of the district is more faithfully preserved.

Whilst the Reformation was spreading in Germany, it was also spreading in Switzerland : as Luther in the one case, so Zwingli in the other, led the van ; and it is noticeable that both champions were born during the same winter (A.D. 1483-4). Each pursued an independent course ; each having been brought to see the errors of Popery from his own point of view ; each possessing a marked idiosyncrasy of mind, and having been led through a particular path of Providence, appropriate to his character and destiny. In many respects they agreed ; but in one they differed, and this was the occasion of the memorable discussion between them at Marburg. The Landgrave of Hesse, Philip the Magnanimous, who had earnestly taken up the cause of the Reformation, and commenced his friendship with Luther at the Diet of Worms, felt anxious to bring together the two leaders of the reforming movement, with a hope that, by mutual explanations, they might come to an agreement, and stop the mouths of Roman Catholics who taunted them with their differences. But beyond religious considerations there were motives of another kind which influenced the Landgrave in this proceeding; he was anxious for an alliance with the Swiss, and amongst other cities with Strasburg, which had adopted the Zwinglian view of the Lord's Supper,—the object of such an alliance being an organized opposition to the Emperor;—and he saw how important it was to settle, if possible, the ecclesiastical differences between the two parties, in order effectually to cement their political union.

His own town of Marburg having been fixed upon by Philip as the place of meeting, hither came Zwingli and his companions on the 29th of September. They had travelled from Zurich by way of Basle and Strasburg, and had tarried at Strasburg with Canon Matthias Zett, whose wife fondly recorded the circumstance in words illustrative of the simple habits of German people in those days: "I was fourteen days maid and cook when the dear, homely men—Œcolampadius and Zwingli—were here at Strasburg, in the year 1529, in the journey, along with our folks, to Marburg, to meet Dr. Luther." They travelled through forests, across mountains, and along valleys, and reached their destination, escorted by forty Hessian cavaliers. They put up at the first house eastward of the Bears' Well.

Luther, accompanied by Melancthon, Justus Jonas, and other Saxon reformers, made their way by Halle, Saxe-Gotha, and Eisenach, to Marburg, and halted at the hotel of the Bear—Barefoot-friar Street. As soon as the two parties arrived, the Landgrave invited them up to the castle and entertained them during their stay.

The place of their discussion was the object of our pilgrimage; and on the morning after we reached Marburg we again ascended the hilly street, and climbed up to the castle. The winding walk

CASTLE OF MARBURG.

is very pleasant, and leads through gardens up to the castle gate. Passing under an archway, you come upon a spacious esplanade, commanding an extensive prospect of the valley watered by the Lahn. Leaning over a parapet, you look out upon a broad and pleasant landscape of field and flood, with a part of the town nestling at the foot of the eminence on the brow of which the castle rests. The buildings are now used as a penitentiary; but in the days when the Landgrave lived there, the place was an abode of regal splendour, and presented manifold signs of state and magnificence which are absent now.

Philip entertained his clerical guests, we are told, in a manner truly royal. "Ah," said Justus Jonas, as he surveyed the palace, "it is not in honour of the Muses, but in honour of God, and of His Christ, that we are so munificently treated in these forests of Hesse." After dinner the first day, Luther chatted with Œcolampadius and Bucer, treating the former with affection, and playfully reproaching the latter for having adopted the side of Zwingli on the subject of the Lord's Supper, the great point in the approaching debate. In one of the rooms of the castle Zwingli and Melancthon held a preparatory conference: Luther and Œcolampadius did the same in another. This was after the whole party had worshipped together, probably in the antique chapel, which is one of the show rooms of the building.

The hall in which the discussion took place was the Knights' Hall, a large apartment still accessible to visitors. It was being restored when we were there in 1872, and workmen were employed in decorating the walls after a manner rather defective in taste. It has a vaulted roof, Gothic arches, and massive columns, and is capable of containing a large number of persons. About twenty-four auditors were present at the commencement of the debate, but their number afterwards amounted to between fifty and sixty. The Landgrave took a seat, surrounded by his court, but in so plain a dress as not to be distinguishable from other people. At a table were the four chief theologians—Luther and Zwingli, Melancthon and Œcolampadius. Behind them were friends of both parties, including "the pious Snepf, the courageous Bucer, the candid Hedio, the valiant Brentz, the amiable Jonas, the fiery Craton, and Mænus, whose soul was stronger than his body"—to adopt language used respecting them at the time by a poet named Cordus.[1] The Landgrave's Chancellor arose, and began the proceedings with a speech in which he exhorted the members that they should act as had been done on like occasions, when learned men came together who had previously written sharply of each other. He would have them banish from their minds ill-humour and bitterness of feeling. Whoever should do this, he said, would, at the same time, discharge his duty and obtain glory and commendation. Others who disregarded unity would afford evidence against themselves, that the Holy Spirit did not rule their hearts.

At the opening of the debate, Luther took a piece of chalk, and on the velvet table-cover wrote in large letters, "*Hoc est corpus meum*," the text which he adopted as a motto, and urged as a main argument for his opinion relative to the Sacrament. With a vivid imagination, a mystical turn of thought, a training in realistic schools of metaphysics, and a strong predilection for high views of Sacraments akin to those he had learned in the Church of Rome, he contended for a change of the elements of bread and wine; not a change of substance, whilst the outward qualities of bread and wine remain as before, which is the Romanist dogma, but a change taking place beneath outward qualities, so that with the substance of bread and wine there is also present the substance of our Lord's body and blood. "I protest," said Luther, "that I differ from my adversaries with regard to the doctrine of the Lord's Supper, and that I shall always differ from them. Christ has said, 'This is My body.' Let them show me that a body is not a body. I reject reason, common sense, carnal arguments, and mathematical proofs."

[1] D'Aubigné, "Hist. of the Reformation," book xiii. c. vii.

Œcolampadius asserted that there were figures of speech in Scripture, such as the "rock was Christ," " I am the vine," and so on ; and that our Lord's words at the Last Supper were to be figuratively explained.

Luther, adhering to a rigid literalism, exclaimed, "We must pay attention to Him who speaks, not to what is said :" meaning, by that, to forbid all critical inquiry into the signification of terms —certainly an astounding proposition. Then, with a beautiful reverence for Divine authority, he added, "God speaks : men—worms—listen ! God commands : let the world obey. Let us fall down together, and humbly kiss the Word." But immediately afterwards, in defiance of taste and reason, he maintained, " If God should order me to eat dung, I would do it, with the assurance that it would be salutary." "'This is My body.' They are the words of God. If the Lord were to set before me wild apples, and command me to eat them, I should eat them, knowing they would be wholesome for me : and I dare not ask, why ? "

At first the debate was conducted by Luther and Œcolampadius —the latter of whom remarked on the gross and degrading sense put by his antagonists on Divine expressions, and exalted the spiritual above the carnal view of the Sacrament ; but soon Zwingli took up the argument, and quoted passages of Scripture in which a sign is described by the thing signified, and maintained that, considering our Lord's declaration, " The flesh profiteth nothing," we must explain the words touching the Eucharist in a similar manner. It was all in vain. Luther could not be moved from his literal stand-point. Placing his finger on the chalked words he kept repeating, "'This is My body.' The devil himself shall not drive me from that. To seek to understand it is to fall away from the faith." Both disputants began to wax intensely warm. Zwingli insisted on the body of Christ being in heaven, and on the impossibility of the same material substance existing in different places at the same time ; to which Luther strangely replied, " He did not care for mathematics." "There is no question of mathematics here," said Zwingli; "but of St. Paul, who writes to the Philippians, μορφὴν δούλου λαβών." Luther interrupted, "Read it in Latin or in German, not in Greek." "Pardon me," resumed the Swiss; "for twelve years past I have made use of the Greek Testament only." Still, the Saxon's finger continued pointing to the chalked words, "*Hoc est corpus meum*," when Zwingli started up, sprang towards Luther, and, striking the table vehemently, exclaimed, "You maintain then, Doctor, that Christ's body is locally in the Eucharist; for you say that Christ's body is literally there. *There* is an adverb of place. Christ's body exists in a place—if in heaven it is not in the bread." "I repeat," the other sturdily persevered, "that I have nothing to do with mathematical proofs. As soon as the words of consecration are pronounced over the bread, the body is there, however wicked be the priest who pronounces them." "You are thus re-establishing popery," urged Zwingli. "This is not done through the priest's merits, but because of Christ's ordinance," was Luther's reply. "I will not, when Christ's body is in question, hear you speak of a particular place. I absolutely will not."

Afterwards they appealed to the Fathers; and the Swiss cited Augustine as on their side. But Luther had only one argument, or rather one assertion. Seizing the velvet table-cloth, with the words on it, "*Hoc est corpus meum*," he thrust it in the face of the Swiss theologians, crying, "See, see! this is our text; you have not yet driven us from it, as you had boasted; and we care for no other proofs." "If this be the case," concluded Œcolampadius, "we had better leave off the discussion."

To prolong the dispute was useless. Blame rested on both sides. Zwingli, before they met, at Marburg, had written sharply to Luther, accusing him of obstinacy—an accusation which, however just and true, was unwise, because it could only serve to exasperate a man of his temperament. Zwingli was a keen, logical disputant, of a decidedly scientific turn, with little imagination, and disposed to take what Luther would deem rationalistic views: Luther, with his realistic imagination and habits of transcendental thought, glorying in what is mysterious, from the deep conviction that God is a mystery and the universe is a mystery, defied the searching analysis of his opponent; and the two men, therefore, stood wide as the poles asunder. Certainly Zwingli had the best of the argument, and in his most excited moments remained less fiery than his redoubtable antagonist: Luther, it would be dishonest to deny, not only lost temper, but showed himself exceedingly obstinate; declining to argue, he only persisted in dogmatic assertions, which sorely tried the patience of the Helvetians. Yet, whilst condemning Luther, we must strive to understand him, and must remember that at the time his object was to save the Reformation from the charge of countenancing low notions of the sacraments—notions which, in his estimation, were chargeable with a rationalistic tendency.]

Nor let us forget that even apostles failed at times to keep their temper. There was a sharp contention between Paul and Barnabas; and Peter, as rash as he was loving, probably did not very calmly listen to his brother, when he "withstood him to the face because he was to be blamed." Our individual duty with regard to the control of our temper, and the culture of a spirit open to conviction, is one thing; our manner of forming an historical judgment of good men, and their failings, is quite another. In thinking over the story of Luther at Marburg, we at times feel very angry; and then again we turn to such considerations as are now indicated, and attempt to form a dispassionate judgment.

Philip the Magnanimous had brought his friends to Marburg with the hope of getting them to agree to some common confession. He saw, at last, that it was impossible they should do so on the subject of the Lord's Supper. Still, was it not possible to unite to some extent? The Landgrave panted for union: so did the

Swiss. "There is no one upon earth," were the words of Zwingli, addressing the Wittenberg divines, "with whom I more desire to be united than with you." Œcolampadius and Bucer said the same. "Acknowledge them as brothers," continued Philip of Hesse. Now it was that Luther appeared at the greatest disadvantage. "You have a different spirit from ours," he affirmed; "our conscience opposes our receiving you as brethren." Did he mean that he would be friendly towards them as fellow-men, but he would not acknowledge them as brothers and members of Christ's Church? Did he intend to say he had nothing to give them except the universal charity all can claim? Then he showed that he did not possess at the time either an apprehension of the doctrine of Christian union, or any portion of its benign and beautiful spirit. Or did he mean only, that he could not hold Church communion with them on account of their divergence on this subject? In either case his conduct must be regarded as a blot on his history. He did, however, so far relent as to draw up certain articles, expressive of a common belief in the main doctrines of the Gospel; yet, in reference to the matter in dispute, all he would say was, that both parties should cherish more of Christian charity for one another, as far as conscience permitted. He added, "We will all earnestly implore the Lord to condescend by His Spirit to confirm us in the sound doctrine." Such words are capable of a good interpretation—one in accordance with the spirit of Catholic unity, and so the Swiss seem to have accepted them; but there is reason to fear that Luther meant no more than probably he had before expressed, namely, that he would treat his opponents with friendliness and charity, though he did not accord to them the relationship of ecclesiastical brethren. That this was what he meant appears from a letter he wrote to Agricola, on the 12th of October, in which—after speaking of the prince's hospitality, and declaring he was perfectly satisfied that he had vanquished his opponents, whom he describes as unskilful in disputation—he says : "They desired that we should recognise them as brethren (*fratres*); this the prince urges on us to do. But it was not possible. Notwithstanding, we gave them the hand of peace and charity (*pacis et caritatis*) that they might cease from violence of expression, and that each might teach his own opinions without invective, though not without argument."

About the same time, writing to his wife, he tells her the Landgrave wished both parties to recognise each other as brethren in Christ; but he adds, " we want not this, though we are advocates for peace and good will."

Zwingli showed a better spirit; and his prayer at the beginning of the strife deserves transcription: " Fill us, O Creator, God and Father of all, with Thy gracious Spirit, and drive from the minds of both sides all the clouds of misunderstanding and passion, as Thou didst of old force the raging waves of the deluge into the deep by Thy powerful winds, and causedst fruits and plants to the full to spring up and to ripen again on the surface of the all-nourishing earth. . . . Arise, O Christ, Thou glorious Sun of Righteousness, and shine on us with Thy mild rays. Alas! while we strive we forget but too often to wrestle after holiness, which Thou requirest from us all. . . . Preserve us, therefore, O Lord, from such strife, that we may not misuse our powers in them, but turn them with all earnestness to the work of sanctification." [1]

Altogether, on Luther's side, this controversy presents a melancholy aspect; but his relative position to the past should be remembered. There is a great difference between a man going up hill and a man going down; a great difference between the twilight of sunrise and the twilight of sunset. Luther had left the depths of error, and was rising to the heights of truth—the sunshine of God's word was rising, not setting, on his soul. Moreover we see

[1] From the introduction to Zwingli's "*Amica Exegesis*," quoted in Christoffel's "Life of Zwingli," translated by Cochran, p. 369. For the story of the Marburg conference, compare Christoffel with D'Aubigné.

that, wise, good, and great as he might be, he was not infallible; and we must no more bow down to a Reformer at Wittenberg than to a Pope at Rome.

During my visit to the town of Marburg, the shade of another Reformer, not German, but English, ever and anon crossed my path, from the circumstance of his having, in all probability, been a resident in the place at the beginning of the year 1530. In the British Museum is a perfect copy of an English translation of the Pentateuch, bearing, at the end of Genesis, this colophon: "Emprented at Marlborow in the land of Hesse, by me Hans Luft, the yere of oure Lorde MCCCCCXXX, the xvii. dayes of Januarii." This translation is the work of William Tyndale; and, in the judgment of his latest and best biographer, the lamented Mr. Demaus, was wholly printed in the town of Marburg; consequently it may be believed that Tyndale was there at the time correcting the press. I thought of him when passing an ancient hostelry or an old-looking bookseller's shop, and wondered whether Tyndale had crossed the threshold; I scarcely imagined he could have had anything to do with the famous discussion in the Knights' Hall. However, Mr. Demaus, after a careful examination of this obscure portion of Tyndale's history, goes so far as to suppose that Tyndale was "one of the favoured fifty" who were admitted into the halls of the old castle, to be present at the gladiatorial contest in which Luther and Melancthon measured swords with Zwingli and Œcolampadius.

The supposition is not reconcilable with the statement of Foxe, that in the latter part of 1529 Tyndale was at Hamburg. That statement, however, on other grounds, is open to suspicion; and therefore the pleasant association suggested by Mr. Demaus is not incredible. Be the matter as it may, the English Reformer, no doubt, within the walls of the Hessian town, devoted himself to an object akin to Luther's—the Reformation of the Church through a translation of the word of God.

Before leaving the Landgrave's castle a word must be added

respecting the Landgrave himself. There can be no doubt that he took a deep interest in the Reformation, and sought to promote it in his dominions; but it is also certain that he was a man of extremely licentious habits. In 1539 he applied to Luther and other divines to know whether the law of God would justify his taking a second wife whilst the first was living. They replied that polygamy, though allowed under the Old Testament, was not the law of the New; that for the Landgrave to be guilty of bigamy would injure Protestantism; and that he ought to abandon his licentious practices and lead a virtuous life; "but," they added, "if your Highness determines to marry another wife, we conjure you to do so privately, that it may be known only to her, yourself, and a few friends, and be kept a profound secret under the seal of confession."[1] The Landgrave's character, bad as it was, casts no blot on the cause he espoused—for a cause intrinsically good cannot be changed by the conduct of its supporters—but the conduct of this man leaves a stain, and a very dark one, upon his own fame. Nor can the temporizing manner of treating his case adopted by the Reformers be vindicated or excused. They did not, it is true, formally give Philip a licence to live with two women, but by their advice they sanctioned his doing so, if he did not tell anybody: and it is melancholy to discover that at the secret marriage which afterwards took place, Bucer and Melancthon were present. Their conduct proceeded partly from commiseration for one placed in unfavourable domestic circumstances; partly from a desire to keep him on the side of the Reformation for its sake and his own; and partly, perhaps chiefly, from that casuistical habit of looking at moral questions, which they had in early days learned from the Church of Rome. That Church cannot consistently condemn what it still does so much to foster.

[1] The answer is dated December 10, 1539. It is in Latin, but with it, in De Wette's edition of Luther's works, is a copy in German, perhaps the original. This bears no other signatures than those of Luther, Melancthon and Bucer.

XV.

COBURG AND SONNEBERG.

ON the way from Augsburg in 1874, I tarried with my daughters for a couple of nights at Nuremberg, to renew my acquaintance with that queen of cities; to gaze once more on the St. Lorenz Kirche, matchless as a combination of symmetrical architecture, exquisite sculpture, and richly coloured glass; to pause in front of the quaintly carved porch of the Frauen Kirche; and to linger, perhaps for the last time, in the nave of St. Sebald, over the peerless shrine of the patron saint. It was fresh from the cunning hands of Peter Vischer, when Luther passed through Nuremberg on his journey homewards in the autumn of 1518; and with his taste for art, the Reformer would be like enough to visit this wonderful work, and examine its elaborate details. At that time the cause of the Reformation had begun to evoke the sympathies of the citizens, and Nuremberg soon became a centre of Protestant influence. It is known as the home of Pirkheimer, the patrician and scholar; of Link and Osiander, famous preachers of the gospel; of Dietrich, who prepared the Nuremberg liturgy, and figured largely in the business of reform; of Camerarius, the classical scholar and professor;

of Eoban Hess, the elegant poet; and Albert Dürer, the world-known artist. When the latter died, Luther acknowledged an elegy on the sad occasion by saying to the poet,—" As to Dürer, it is a pious act to mourn over the loss of so excellent a man. But it is yours to pronounce him happy, that Christ hath taken him away so well prepared, and by so peaceful an end, from times so turbulent;

THE HIMMELSTHOR, NUREMBERG CASTLE.

and to be perhaps more turbulent still, lest he who was worthy of the happiest times should live to see the most wretched. Let him rest in peace, then, with his fathers." It adds to the interest of a walk to the gravestone in St. John's Cemetery of the immortal painter and engraver, to remember these words, which entwine in loving Christian bonds two names which shed such different rays of lustre on the age in which they lived.

Upon reaching Coburg we immediately arranged a trip to Sonneberg, which we wished to see before we went up to the castle where Luther stayed during the Augsburg Diet of 1530. Sonneberg has just acquired a connection with Luther through the removal to the neighbourhood of a wooden building used as an inn, formerly belonging to a place called Judenbach. The removal was owing to the liberality of a gentleman at Sonneberg, who determined to save the relic, when on the point of being pulled down and knocked

GRAVE OF ALBERT DÜRER.

to pieces. He had it transported to the spot where it now appears, restored to its pristine condition. The reopening of the inn was the occasion of a festival at the beginning of August, 1874, which attracted much attention in Germany and England. Unfortunately I could not reach Sonneberg until a fortnight afterwards.

The journey by rail from Coburg to Sonneberg, occupying less than an hour, is through a district of plain and valley, swelling up into gentle hills, the landscape being covered with open fields, relieved now and then by a thriving village or a wide stretch of pine wood. When we reached the end of our journey we inquired

after the Luther house, and were pointed to a dark brown spot on the slope of a green hill lying on the other side of the town.

Sonneberg is a nest of toy-makers, living in clean, comfortable houses, with tokens of their craft at every turn and corner. A sign on a building to the effect that it was "a manufactory of crying babies" was one of the first objects which attracted our attention. Wooden horses were poking their heads out of open windows, through which you could see a woman with a paint-brush ready to make the steed she held in her hand red or black, grey or spotted; another was whisking liliputian tails, whilst a man adorned a rocking-horse with the gayest trappings. There are several winding streets in the town, a good many shops of a humble description, and on the outskirts some very cosy residences with gardens. Passing by a newly built church we reached the Luther house, near which lingered a solitary relic of the recent doings,—an inscription within a wreath of faded leaves, affectionately welcoming "all dear comers to the Luther feast."

The house stands on a grassy slope not far from an extensive fir plantation. The town is seen nestling close by, and villages, cottages, and groups of trees are scattered around amidst smiling fields. The house is a specimen of the roadway inn of three or four centuries ago, a sort of log hut, with tall slanting roof, little windows, and a sign hanging over the door. The new one exhibits the words "*Zum Dr. Martin Luther,*" with the picture of a host offering good cheer to the traveller. Inside there are three rooms on the ground floor: on the left hand, one containing a German stove, two tables, and benches with shelves over them bearing jugs, drinking-cups, and glasses: behind, and opening into it, is a very small bedroom, and on the right hand a third apartment, which remains unfurnished. The restoration has been executed with taste and judgment.

Judenbach, where the house formerly stood, is about an hour and a quarter's drive from Sonneberg, on the top of a hill 2,000 feet above the level of the sea. The straggling village is inhabited by people who cut wood for the Sonneberg toy-makers, and make inferior goods for their market. It occupies a point on the great high road which in the Middle Ages carried the trade and traffic of the south through the Forest of Thuringia to the central Erfurt mart, and to the courtly town of Saxe Weimar. Martin Luther travelled along that road in 1518, tarrying at the inn on his way from Wittenberg to Heidelberg; and he makes reference to the village of Judenbach in a letter written the 15th of April on his arrival at Coburg. He met, as he tells his friend Spalatin, under the humble roof the Electoral Councillor Pfeffinger, who paid 10 groschen for the entertainment of the Reformer and his companions. From the same letter we learn that Luther performed his journey on foot, "very much wearied." On his return from this journey he fared better, for he relates, in a letter dated May 18, that he travelled home in a carriage from Nuremberg to Würzburg, and thence to Erfurt with the brethren of that place.

A still more important visit was paid by the Reformer to the Judenbach inn on the 14th of April, 1530, as he was on his way to Coburg, to tarry at the castle during the Augsburg Diet. The visit is described in a record of the events connected with the inn, published and circulated at the Luther Festival, under the title of *Chronica von Judenbach.*

" Elector John the Steadfast came here with Dr. Martin Luther on his way to the Diet at Augsburg. In his train were the Electoral Prince Johann Friedrich, Prince Wolfgang of Anhalt, Duke Franz of Lüneberg, Counts Albrecht and Jobst, of Mansfeld ; Count Ernst of Gleichen; five Electoral Councillors ; Chancellors Brueck and Baïer; besides Dr. Luther, Melancthon, Justus Jonas, and Spalatin, and seventy nobles, with one hundred and sixty mounted body-men (all furnished with firearms, and clad in dress of leather). The party reached Coburg on the 15th of April, where Dr. Luther remained in the fortress. On the 5th of October of the same year the Elector and his train returned, bringing with them Luther from Coburg."

Having understood that, besides the *Judenbach Chronicle*, a number of other small publications and fly-sheets were issued in connection with the festival, I was anxious to obtain a collection of them, and therefore applied at two or three bookshops. Nowhere could I get what I wanted. But at the railway station, when one of our number represented our disappointment to the station-master, he placed a packet of them in my hands to look at on our way back to Coburg. An offer made to purchase the collection was declined, but when he understood what I wanted them for, he politely presented the whole for my acceptance. The recent festival, he said, had been a great success. A train of twenty railway carriages had brought visitors from a distance; neighbouring towns and villages had poured out their inhabitants, and at least ten thousand people altogether had assembled. He noticed with pride, that correspondents of the "Times" and the "Daily News" had been attracted to the spot to describe the incidents of this commemorative gathering. And I am glad of an opportunity to record my obligations to a gentleman belonging to a class, who by their friendly offers do so much in a quiet way to promote real brotherhood between the people of one nation and another.

The packet contained twenty-six publications of different kinds, some printed in old type, and on paper made expressly for the purpose, so as to present accurate specimens of old books and handbills. Among them is the *Chronica von Judenbach* already mentioned, giving a summary of notable incidents connected with the place from the year 1457 to the year 1870, under which last date, it is stated that fifteen young men of the village were engaged in the war with France. "One was missing, two were wounded, and the rest returned safe and sound." I find also verses and hymns for the festival, especially a facsimile of the famous "*Ein' feste Burg ist unser Gott*," set to music in Luther's own handwriting.

Amongst copies of indulgences, one ornamented with the papal keys and triple crown reads as follows:

"In the authority of all the saints, and in compassion towards thee, I absolve thee from all sins and misdeeds, and remit all punishment for ten days.

"JOHANNES TIETZEL."

Another and more valuable is entitled, "Indulgence: in nomine Papæ: for the entire life:"[1]

"I, by virtue of the apostolic power entrusted to me, do absolve thee from all ecclesiastical censures, judgments, and punishments which thou must have merited; besides this, from all excesses, sins, and crimes thou mayest have committed, however great and shameful they may have been, and for whatever cause, even in those cases reserved for our most Holy Father the Pope. I obliterate every taint of unvirtues, all signs of infamy, which thou mayest have received. I release thee from all punishments which thou wouldst have endured in purgatory. I permit thee again to participate in the sacraments of the Church. I incorporate thee again in the community of the sanctified, and replace thee in the state of innocence and purity in which thou wert at the hour of thy baptism. So that in the moment of thy death, the door through which the sinner enters the place of torture and punishment will be closed, and that will be open to thee which leads into the paradise of joys. If thou shouldst not soon die, so shall this grace remain unshakable until the end of thy life. In the name of the Holy Father. Amen.

"JOHANN TIETZEL, Apostol. Commissarius."

Not having witnessed the festival itself, I insert an interesting account of it given by a correspondent who noted what he saw from hour to hour.

[1] I have adopted the translation in the "Daily News."

Ablaß:

In nomine Papae, auf Lebzeit.

Ich, kraft der mir anvertrauten apostolischen Macht, spreche dich los von allen geistlichen Censuren, Urtheilssprüchen und Strafen, die du verdient hast, überdies von allen von dir begangenen Excessen, Sünden und Verbrechen, wie groß und schändlich sie auch sein mögen und um welch Sach willen es auch sei, auch für die unserm allerheiligsten Vater dem Papste reservirten Fälle.

Ich lösche jeglichen Makel der Untüchtigkeit, alle Zeichen der Ehrlosigkeit aus, die du dabei erhalten haben magst. Ich erlasse dir die Strafen, die du im Fegfeuer hättest erdulden müssen. Ich gestatte dir wieder die Theilnahme an den kirchlichen Sakramenten.

Ich einverleibe dich wieder der Gemeinschaft der Heiligen und setze dich in die Unschuld und Reinheit zurück, in der du zur Stunde deiner Taufe gewesen bist. So, daß im Augenblick deines Todes das Thor, durch welches man in den Ort der Qualen und Strafen eingeht, verschlossen bleibt und jenes sich aufthut, welches zum Paradies der Freude führt. Solltest du nicht bald sterben, so bleibt diese Gnade unerschütterlich bis zu deinem Lebensende.

Im Namen des heiligen Vaters, Amen.

Johann Tetzel,
apostol. Commissarius.

"The festival proper began at two in the afternoon, by the representation on the hillside of an annual village fair and *fête*, such as we may see in German villages to this day, but with the difference that the booths and wares and costumes of the sellers were characteristic of the Reformation era. It was a busy, thriving time, and the delineators took their parts with great spirit and humour. You could purchase at one stall coarse blue, green, and yellow stuff to clothe your spearmen and escort, and helmets to protect them in such rows as they were liable to get into with Tetzel and his assistants. At another you could purchase leathern articles straps and saddles, and 'Luther soles,' with the inscription, 'Whoever possesses such soles does not need to buy any indulgences.' Then another with scythes and sickles, and another still with boots, such as the people of Luther's time must have worn, shoes of leather and shoes of wood, the latter being of the same pattern as those worn by peasants in some parts of Germany to this day. The proprietor of this stall was the best character, I think, of the fair, a veritable Hans Sach, quaint in looks and in costume, and in his sayings, and jolly and humorous in his dealings with his modern customers. Then there were booths for the sale of antique toys, kept by pretty rosy-cheeked Thuringian maidens, picturesquely clad in all the colours of the rainbow, and the high 'white cotton nightcap' head-dresses of long ago. An interesting booth was the 'menagerie,' with great paintings of elephants and lions and tigers in front, and two immense negro heads with tongues out-lolling, placed at each corner, and over the doorway five or six youthful musicians in the most outrageously chosen costumes, discoursing wild music, from the Lutheran era, I suppose, to attract the peasants thirsting for natural historical knowledge. Paying six kreuzers, I entered and found a most interesting collection of owls, descendants of similar birds that possibly screeched about the time Tetzel was wandering through Germany on his interesting tour. Then the veritable brother of "Dr. Eisenbart, who cureth ills of every sort,' had planted a booth for the sale of his miraculous elixirs, kept in immense jars and tiny phials. Dr. Eisenbart was a wild-looking individual, clad in red hose and a green jerkin with red arms, and on his head a red and white striped nondescript horn-of-plenty cap, who eulogized his wares with great volubility, relating to us terrible stories of the wondrous cures he had performed on sick persons, alive and dead.

"Such may have been a village fair in the days of Luther. At such a time, when the people from the neighbouring villages and mountains would naturally flock to Judenbach to see all the wondrous sights therein gathered, it was also very natural that either Monsieur Tetzel or some of his assistants should honour the place and the people with a visit, needful as the latter were for the means of gaining eternal bliss. And a scene very characteristic was delineated yesterday afternoon. Immediately in front of the Luther House a rude pulpit had been erected, in which the representative of the veritable Tetzel gesticulated violently, and urged the people, with loud voice and coarse jests, to purchase his letters of indulgence and introduction to the heavenly regions. On one side of the pulpit an immense red cross had been planted, and on the other a papal standard, while in front a coarse-featured peasant held up the papal bull which authorized Tetzel's labours. Immediately in front of the pulpit, lower down the hill, were seated at a long wooden table two of Tetzel's monk secretaries, one dealing out the indulgences to the many monk assistants, who disposed of them among the people, while another, clad in the garb of the Dominicans, was seated behind a huge chest in which he deposited the money brought in by the assistants. The money-chest was ornamented with small gilded pictures, representing poor souls tormented by Satan in purgatory, and bore the well-known inscription in German,—

> 'The moment the money in the box doth ring,
> The soul out of purgatory to heaven doth spring.'

Some half-score of monks of various orders darted hither and thither among the people, selling their wares with great rapidity. First Tetzel would utter a discourse to attract the crowds away from the other shows of the fair, from Dr. Eisenbart and the menagerie of owls; and then, after his rude banter and coarse jests, his emissaries would distribute themselves over the ground, offering their indulgences of various degrees, shouting but one word, 'Buy! buy! buy!' Tetzel's address could be purchased in printed form under the title,—

"'This is the address of the Doctor Johann Tietzel, who, with the knowledge and will of the Pope and the Holy Curia at Rome, doth visit the annual mart at Judenbach.'

"'Come here! come here! he cried out, 'ye great and small, rich and poor, thick and thin; ye will all go to the devil unless you receive grace at my hands.' He went on to charge the people with all the crimes of the Decalogue,—

"'Cursing, quarrelling, blaspheming, lying, backbiting, slandering, deceiving, debt-making, gluttony, and drunkenness;'

and urged them to get grace for all their sins by purchasing his indulgences.

"'If any one hath committed murder' (he says) 'it will cost twenty guldens; if he hath stolen, it will cost but twenty groschen; if he hath set fire to his mother-in-law he can get free from guilt for five groschen;—then will he be as pure as a diamond, as a new-born child.'

He concluded his fiery address something in the following style:

"'Oh, see, my favours are so cheap;
Now grasp into your purses deep;
And he who goes the deepest down
Shall wear in heaven the brightest crown.
Quando sonat pecunia,
The moment money i' th' box doth ring,
In cœlum salit anima,
The soul straightway to heaven doth spring.
Indulgences—oh buy! oh buy!
Then you can get to heaven so high,
Where all the little angels dear
Do sing with voices fine and clear;
No torturing fires do there annoy—
There you may sit in lasting joy,'" etc., etc.

In another division of the dispatch the correspondent adds,—

"It is now about half-past three in the afternoon, and Tetzel and his monks have been labouring hard for fully two hours. Tetzel himself (represented by Theodore Neumann, a bookbinder of Sonneberg), a man of swarthy features and clad in the garb of the Dominicans, is almost hoarse with shouting, and his assistants still go at their work in a silent, bull-dog fashion. Suddenly a noise is heard away down at the foot of the hill, at the entrance to the village; we hear shouting and the voices of children singing, and a herald and mounted lancebearers come in sight, and we know that Dr. Martin Luther is about to enter the little village of Judenbach. More men of the mounted escort belonging to Elector John, and then a simple peasant waggon, decorated with branches of trees, drawn by huge, wondrously quaint-caparisoned horses, and driven by huge-booted drivers. In it are seated four men in black clerical gowns and caps, and we know at a glance that the face of the one in front belongs to sturdy, honest, God-fearing, Satan-defying Martin Luther. There is no mistaking the likeness. The other occupants of the waggon are Melancthon, Justus Jonas, and others. The mounted escort rides ahead, through the throng of the fair, up to the Luther House; the waggon is halted, and the great Reformer and his friends alight, and gaze upon the scenes before them with anger and astonishment. Hardly before we have time to grasp the scene, a contest ensues between Luther's escort, assisted by the people, and Tetzel and his monks. Tetzel sees his danger, and, hard pressed, he seizes the large red cross, and bidding his secretaries secure the treasury and the other paraphernalia of his mission, starts to flee through the crowd. They are followed by some of the escort. The people hoot and yell with delight. Suddenly Tetzel is for a moment brought to bay. The escort have secured the treasury, and the Dominican turns round fiercely upon his pursuers, and swinging the huge red cross about him, and supported by his monks with their staffs, and some peasants with stout sticks, makes a good defence. Thus the conflict continues until the foot of the hill is reached; Tetzel and his monks disappear among the houses of the village, and the escort bring back their treasure in triumph, cheered by the assembled people. The escort then return to their comrades, who are bivouacking further up the hill. They present a picturesque scene: the men in bright particoloured costumes, the horses gaily decked out, and all artistically grouped. The *Lanzknechts* burnish their spears, and the mounted men of the escort caress and feed their steeds.

"Another picture. In the corner of the paled enclosure in front of the Luther House the great Reformer has watched the flight of the monks; and the faces of the vast crowds are now turned up to him, expecting that he will address them. And in clear, forcible words, in strong contrast with the ribaldry of Tetzel, the Reformer's voice is heard by even the most distant of the audience, and his words are most attentively listened to. [This address is an interesting document, and was prepared for the occasion by an eminent Lutheran theologian.] Some parts of it are especially telling:—

"'Beloved people and evangelical brethren,' he commences, 'again I see before me the good people of Thuringia, free like its forests, and joyous in its God and in its faith. Ye have purified your hearts, and have put away all that is contrary to the true faith in God. What those people' (referring to the retreating monks) 'preach and teach is not of the kingdom of heaven, but of the kingdom of the devil. Long enough has the Pope taught the doctrine—Go to Rome, get indulgences, confess, and do penance, exercise yourselves in the service of the saints, and mortify the flesh. And monks, nuns, and priests have boasted that they were the servants of God and the brides of Christ; but they all lack the proper way, and the *Evangelium* is unknown to them. Whoever preaches to you must be a true preacher, who shall fulfil his office faithfully; he must boldly utter the truth to all, whether they be poor or rich, small or powerful, friend or foe. And he shall speak freely and openly. For whoever would be a light shall not creep into the corner, but stand out boldly upon the market-place, and be undaunted.

"Very effective is the passage in which he speaks of his life in Thuringia:

"'So do I stand here openly before you—here on the borders of my beloved Thuringia, on whose mountains, with their fresh green firs and their murmuring beeches, on whose manly, hospitable people the heart doth verily rejoice. Here is the heart open and the mind clear. Yea, am I not a child of this people of Thuringia, grown up in its mountain freshness, educated in its ancient city of Eisenach, and steeled in theological sufferings and struggles in its monastic town of Erfurt? Did not old Wartburg there in the west, give me protection from the lurking foe? Do I not see before me there, in the south, the high fortress of Coburg, that seems to beckon to me, offering me a sure place of safety whenever my adversaries shall persecute me anew? Have I not friends and co-fighters in plenty here in the lands of Thuringia? and is not the Thuringian people truly devoted to me in pure zeal and pious faith, convinced that it is the true light which driveth away and scareth off the black deeds of the Antichrist? And just here, close to the borders wherein the little Pope in Bamberg still carries on his monkish doings, and sends out his myrmidons and ensnarers to persuade the people with their brotherhoods, prayers, rosaries, pilgrimages, and indulgence papers, is a most important and necessary stronghold of the faith. Therefore be steadfast, and be of firm will to place body and possessions in the scale for the upholding of the *Evangelium*.'

"Thus he went on urging the people to abide strong in the new faith, concluding with the words,—

"'I know this people as myself, and know that it will victoriously oppose all Papacy and Romanism. And if the day come when it is necessary for all to stand united against anti-christian foes and adversaries who skulk about in the empire and destroy the growing seed, then stand firm as one man, and remain true to your God and your faith. Farewell, beloved and evangelical countrymen, be joyous in faith, and put your trust in God now and for evermore. And when I am no longer with you, and children and children's children look back upon our days, which will bring forth a new era, then be assured that our work will still live on and on; we must at last succeed! Yea, e'en were the foe e'er so many, God will maintain the field. Amen.'

"Then the Reformer turned to listen to the songs of the village school children who had gathered around him, and when they commenced the well-known strains of the grand old choral, Luther himself joined in with sturdy lungs, and then the people around him, until the ten thousand guests assembled on the hillside helped to swell the mighty soul-stirring chorus, '*Ein' feste Burg ist unser Gott*,' and the mountains around us joined in too, as is their wont in this part of the world, and echoed back the solemn strains that Luther composed centuries ago in that high fortress of strength that we can see with the naked eye from where we thousands stand. Seldom has Thuringia heard the grand old

COURTYARD OF COBURG CASTLE.

choral so magnificently rendered. It was a fitting and solemn closing to a festival which, with all its earnest motives, furnished so much material for amusement."[1]

We returned to Coburg in the evening, and took a moonlight ramble through the town and round the outskirts. The agreeable impression then received was deepened the next day. The market-place, surrounded by buildings of quaint architecture, contains in the middle a bronze statue of the late Prince Consort of England, executed after a design by my friend Mr. Theed, a sculptor of whom England may be proud: the ceremony of its being unveiled by our gracious Queen was an incident which lives in the memory of the inhabitants of the town.

The palace called Ehrenburg is famous for the Riesensaal, or Giant Hall, with rows of immense caryatides on either side, for a valuable collection of engravings, and for choice specimens of marqueterie, in the manufacture of which the artizans of Coburg are said to excel. The arsenal contains curious armour and proud trophies, and the architecture of the streets will gratify the traveller who has an eye for what is picturesque and quaint. But the castle is the main attraction. It stands on a lofty hill, the ascent of which is a heavy pull. Near the top is an extensive view, embracing open country of the same character as seen from Sonneberg. Indeed, Sonneberg lies right before you to the north-east.

The castle is surrounded by a moat, now dry and turned into a garden, and the gateway exhibits an ancient portcullis. The ducal arms are carved in stone on a corner battlement; and entering a small courtyard, with a canopied well in the centre, you are in front of a picturesque range of buildings, with a gallery running across, under a line of windows cut in a wall of cross-patterned timber-work. Virginian creepers, in graceful festoons, cling round the porch and gallery, and the whole place has a charming sylvan

[1] "Daily News," August 5th and 6th.

air. Having ascended the steps to a rustic gallery, you are amused by a fresco representing a bridal procession in the olden times.

The guide conducts his visitors into a large rambling place full of old coaches—one a Brautwagen of 1527, framed of wood and huge hoops, a vehicle such as Martin Luther might have occupied on his journey from Coburg to Erfurt. Then come a succession of apartments in an upper story, to which you ascend by an old

CASTLE OF COBURG.

staircase adorned with paintings and armour. In these apartments are specimens of antique furniture—china, pottery, and glass,— such as interest the connoisseur in works of old world art. The Reformation has many mementos on the walls in portraits of Luther and Catherine von Bora, of Melancthon, and other Protestant celebrities, some being painted on gold so as to produce a rich effect. The castle contains besides, a splendid armory, filled with suits of steel and iron, and exhibiting, by means of a skilful arrangement of figures, a very good representation of a tournament on horseback.

Luther was conducted to this castle in April, 1530, as appears from the *Judenbach Chronicle*, by the Elector John the Steadfast, to whom the castle at that time belonged, and who wished to have him both within his own reach and out of harm's way during the Augsburg Diet. Luther had one companion, his friend Dietrich, a native of Nuremberg, a rising theologian, who had accompanied Luther to Marburg, and who, after living fourteen years at Wittenberg in close connection with him, returned to Nuremberg, and took a leading part in promoting the Reformation there.

The Reformer, as he rambled through the empty rooms and the forsaken courts, suffered much from depression, and that troublesome noise in his head of which he often complained. For a time without books and papers, he seems to have compensated for a little transient leisure by applying himself to the translation of the prophecies, the composition of sermons and treatises, and the study of theological subjects for decision at Augsburg, under Melancthon's management.

The entrance into Luther's rooms is from the hall at the foot of the staircase. They are situated on the left-hand side of the entrance to the castle. The Reformer's sitting-room is square, small, and wainscoted, with two little windows in recesses, furnished with seats on both sides. There is a case against the wall containing a collection of Bibles and of Luther's works; and in the middle of the apartment is a table, with a chair such as the Reformer might have used. Figures, busts, a Luther jug, and the inevitable German stove, complete the furniture.

It is stated in the letterpress descriptions appended to the charming views of the ducal palaces of Saxe-Coburg and Gotha by Douglas Morison, that here Luther wrote his immortal song, '*Eine feste burg ist unser Gott*," a statement which needs to be modified by remembering what is said on a former page.[1] I have no doubt that the writer has the authority of local tradition for what he records; and it may be taken in proof that the hymn which embodies the sentiment of Luther's life here received its finishing touches.

It is added in the volume on the ducal palaces that he inscribed the walls of his room "with several sentences expressive of his trials and his constancy:" among these are cited "I shall not die, but live, and declare the works of the Lord;" "The way of the wicked shall perish;" "It tarries long, but wait."

Luther's sleeping chamber adjoins his sitting-room, it has one window and a little window-seat. Only a fragment of the Reformer's bedstead remains.

Here Luther wrote a number of letters, one on the 22nd of April, in which he tells Melancthon that the Sinai of Coburg was a Zion, and that he would build there three tabernacles—one for the Psalms, one for the prophets, and one for the fables of Æsop; remarking that the whole fortress with all the keys had been entrusted to him; that there were more than thirty persons within the walls, of whom twelve were night guards and two were watchmen on different towers. Another on the same day to Justus Jonas, contained the well-known fable of the birds:—There was directly before his window in the castle a grove, where another diet was being held, composed of rooks, that made an immense hubbub night and day. The nobles and great ones—he had not seen their emperor—were frisking about, not gaily attired, but all in black clothes, with grey eyes, singing the same song in a palace hall, which had the blue sky for a ceiling, the ground for a floor, green branches for panelling, and the ends of the earth for walls. They had no horses and waggons, but meditated a crusade against wheat, barley, and all kinds of corn. He considered them Papists, to whose preaching

[1] See page 118.

he was forced to listen, as they devoured the produce of the earth and cackled for it beforehand.

In the month of May he wrote a touching letter of condolence to Justus Jonas on the death of his child. The next month Luther's father died, "sweetly falling asleep, strong in the faith of Christ." The son wrote, that he now succeeded to the seniorship of the family, that it became him to mourn for one who had toiled for his support, and that he rejoiced to know his parent had lived in days when he could see the light of divine truth. On the 18th of June he complained of his chronic trouble, a thundering noise in his head; but he was hard at work completing his translation of Ezekiel, and beginning the translation of the other prophets. At the end of the month he was still at work upon the Bible, as well as upon a criticism of Melancthon's Augsburg Confession. Other letters follow, in one of which he said he hoped and feared a whole forest of epistles from his friends, more numerous and obstreperous than the birds by the castle window.

Murray's guide book states that the pulpit from which Luther preached in the curious old chapel is shown. Such is not now the case. The chapel is dismantled, with a view to its restoration, and at present contains nothing curious; the only interest attaching to it is, in the fact, that here he delivered some of his sermons, the drift and spirit of which may be conjectured from the following passage in a letter, dated June 20, "I have here become a new pupil of the Decalogue, and am making myself a boy again, and learning it by heart. I begin to consider the Decalogue as the logic of the Gospel, and the Gospel as the rhetoric of the Decalogue: and Christ as having all that is in Moses, but Moses as not having all that is in Christ."

XVI.

THE TOWN AND LEAGUE OF SCHMALKALDEN.

EVERYBODY who has dipped into the history of the German Reformation has met with the name of Schmalkalden; but few perhaps can tell exactly where it is. We must confess that for a good while it was to us a *terra incognita*, beyond some vague idea of its being an old town in the heart of Thuringia. In connection with Martin Luther it crops up distinctly; and any one inquisitive about his life must feel curiosity as to the exact situation and the present appearance of this odd-named locality.

Whilst tarrying at Eisenach, I found that Schmalkalden was not more than between twenty and thirty English miles distant, and easily accessible by railway. Therefore I determined to pay a visit to the place, and on a bright August morning started on an expedition. Schmalkalden lies to the south of Eisenach, and to the east of Wernhausen, a station on the Coburg line, whence there runs a branch to the town geographically obscure, but historically famous. The ride is exceedingly pleasant, through a country which exhibits bewitching intricacies of hill and dale, of abounding woods and of trickling waters. Villages are seen nestling in quiet nooks, bulbous church spires peer above the trees, and breadths of corn and tobacco land outspread themselves far and wide, with the Thuringian high lands in the distance. Now comes a ravine full of oaks and pines leading up to the castle walls, then cliffs of light red sandstone follow, draped with ferns, trailing plants, and wild flowers. Nor does the region strike one as at all out of the way of the world, for plenty of people await the arrival of the train at the stations, and in one case the platform was crowded with passengers.

Arrived at my destination, I found in all directions agreeable views, meadows, gardens, and green hills, with a straggling town in front, and a white palatial-looking mansion, the Electoral Castle of Wilhelmsburg, on the right-hand side.

On entering the town I noticed an old-fashioned house, bearing this inscription over the doorway,—

> "Whoever passes through this door
> Should keep in mind for evermore,
> That holy Jesus Christ is given
> To be the only door to heaven."

The religious spirit breathed through this German doggerel is in accordance with some allegorical figures on another house, answering to the words *pietas* and *fides*. Further on attention is arrested by a lion upholding a shield, brilliantly painted and gilded, and marked by the date 1583. Quaintness and antiquity are stamped on all the dwellings, and the further you advance the more striking becomes the aspect of the place. Often in German towns most of the domestic architecture is ancient, yet modern innovation is manifest in many directions. But in Schmalkalden the visitor walks up and down street after street without meeting with a single tenement looking less than two or three centuries old. It is the kind of place that would have thrown Scott or Prout into raptures, suggesting old-world descriptions to the one and affording picturesque sketches to the other.

Timber houses are universal, with great dark wooden beams thrown out in bold relief by white plaster in the intermediate walls; coats of arms are exhibited over doors, bright flowers in pots and baskets adorn the windows, pretty little gardens are numerous. Trees and shrubs overhang the walls, the Virginia creeper abounds, streams of water flow down the sides of the streets, crossed by tiny stone bridges, and enlivened by numbers of ducks. Fowls pick round the doorways and are allowed free ingress and egress. Waggons drawn by oxen lumber over the rough pavement, and women in provincial costume—white sleeves, dark petticoats, an ugly cloak, and an ugly skull-cap—carry on their backs long tubs and heavy baskets. A friendly spirit pervades the region, and the stranger is saluted with civil nods from heads peeping out of doorways and windows.

Schmalkalden is a great smithy. Iron ore is supplied from numerous mines in the neighbourhood. The people are chiefly employed in working metals. You hear everywhere strokes of the hammer and raspings of the file. Window after window exhibits articles in tin, brass, and iron; yet the town wears no black begrimed appearance. On the contrary, it is well kept and clean; on a summer's day it is bright and cheerful. Indeed, looking simply at its street architecture, and the old-fashioned air which every object assumes, it is in itself worthy of a visit. If you wish to put back for a day the clock of time, and to spend a few hours in the sixteenth century, go to Schmalkalden.

The two chief hotels are *Gasthof zur Adler*, a very old straggling edifice with a courtyard and large hall which might have served for a baronial castle; and *Gasthof zur Krone* just opposite, where we begin to light upon Lutheran associations. "Dem andenken," says an inscription on the wall, " Dr. Martin Luther, gevichmet Stadt Schmalkalden, am 31 October, 1817." This memorial of the Reformer, placed there in the year 1817, the tercentenary of the commencement of his grand career, leads to inquiries respecting the house on which the words are inscribed and it is soon discovered that this is no other than the building in which the famous Schmalkalden League was concerted and commenced in the year 1531.

The perils of the Protestant cause had appeared very plainly at the Diet of Augsburg in 1530. The Emperor Charles V. had refused to accept the apology then and there presented by the Reformers. The rising church of Luther and Melancthon was threatened with extermination. Legal processes were prepared against the states which had confiscated Roman Catholic property. The princes and representatives of the most powerful cities on the side of the Reformation, with the Elector of Saxony and the Landgrave of Hesse at their head, felt the time was come for them to stand on their defence; accordingly they assembled in Schmalkalden, being a central town within the dominions of the latter potentate. In great religious movements political elements are sure to commingle, and in this instance distinguished persons, dissatisfied with the imperial Government on different grounds, combined with the Protestant princes against the Emperor. The King of Bavaria, a thorough Roman Catholic, did so because he was displeased at the appointment of Ferdinand, Charles's brother, as King of the Romans. Thus princely electors assembled in this Thuringian town, March 29, 1531. Hither they rode in the early spring, under leafless trees and budding hedges, cased in armour, with banners and squires, and troops of attendants, dappling the road with an array of brilliant colours, amidst which gleamed in early sunshine the crested casque and noble lance of knightly soldiers, and the humble steel caps and weapons of men-at-arms. They poured into the place as the streets were lined with townspeople, and women and children gazed out of the windows upon the long array, which meant a good deal more than it was in the power of spectators to understand.

The grandees alighted at the door of what is now the "Guest

house of the Crown," and under its roof they carried on their weighty deliberations. Upon my inquiring whether any particular room could be identified as the scene of the transaction, the landlord conducted me up an old-fashioned staircase to a large apartment, still retaining an antique look, which he stated was once occupied by the great men who planned the league. And just as I was leaving the spot he stepped into a smaller room close by, full of lumber, out of which he brought a walking-stick, said to have belonged to Martin Luther. So potent was the effect of the league in the mind of the Emperor, just at the time when his dominions were threatened by the Turks, and the Sultan Solyman was pushing towards the Danube, that he showed himself disposed to make concessions; and in the month of July, 1532, concluded in the city of Nuremberg, religious peace with the Protestant powers, parties on both sides agreeing to suspend hostilities until a general council could be held.

But the Schmalkalden League was only for a while suspended by this arrangement.

We find it afterwards in active operation, greatly invigorated by fresh accessions of strength. In 1535 there was another meeting in the same place, attended by English as well as German representatives. Dr. Barnes was then envoy of Henry VIII. together with Edward Fox, Bishop of Hereford, and Archdeacon Heath. They came with a floating idea of some great alliance, in which Germany and England might strengthen one another's hands in the good fight of faith. Subsequently overtures were made to Henry to accept the headship of a reforming confederacy, based on the Augsburg confession, which of course came to nothing. However, to an Englishman visiting Schmalkalden it is interesting to think of the ecclesiastics from his own country having once walked these streets, and having sat in that big old room in the Crown Hotel, debating questions of life and death.

The league at last led to a war, and under the years 1546 and

1547 the pages of German history are reddened and blackened by the blood and smoke of a battle in the forest of Lochan, near Muhlberg, where the poor Landgrave of Hesse had to surrender at discretion, and the Reformation, on its political side, received a terrible blow.

I walked about in quest of a house more interesting than the Crown Hotel, called the *Sannersche Haus*, where Luther and others in 1537 drew up certain theological articles, which became identified with the political league. Wandering up a street opposite to the hotel I reached a bookseller's shop, with photographs and engravings in the window, and having made some purchases, proceeded to inquire for the *Sannersche Haus*. "Here is the very place," exclaimed the worthy tradesman; and finding I was employed on a Lutheran pilgrimage, he courteously invited me to enter his dwelling. We ascended a rather grand old oak staircase, which conducted to a spacious landing-place, the walls of which were decorated with emblems in plaster of the four seasons of the year, probably belonging to the sixteenth century. There opened upon it a handsome drawing-room, with a richly plastered ceiling of the same age. This my informant declared to be the room in which Luther lodged during his stay at Schmalkalden, where he held his consultations with Melancthon and others, and where he drew up the world-known articles. This, as I afterwards saw, is notified by an inscription outside the dwelling, in connection with the figure of Luther's swan.

The room contains modern furniture and has a cosy appearance, and I felt much interested in a small early printed volume in the possession of the bookseller, which he showed with no little pride, containing Luther's autograph. A smaller adjoining apartment, somewhat altered from what it was originally, is called Luther's bedchamber, where, at the time I entered it, there lay a sleeping infant in its little cot, not far from its mother's side. These rooms must detain us for a moment, as it is worth while to remember the opinion of Luther respecting the league, the nature of the articles he drew up, and certain personal incidents which occurred during his visit.

Luther had strong scruples with regard to the warlike character of the combination. He did not approve of an appeal to arms in support of religion, but preferred to trust to moral influences; though he did not oppose legislative enactments in its behalf, or refuse to accept for its propagation aid out of State resources. Through the counsels and persuasions of learned jurists, however, he became reconciled to the idea of a compact among the princes for carrying out their ecclesiastical designs, since he was assured this was perfectly constitutional, inasmuch as the Emperor was bound by the principles on which his government was based, not to infringe on the laws of the State or the liberties of the Germanic Church. Still he was averse to unsheathing the sword against the Emperor, for whose office he felt the deepest reverence, and whose authority, as far as possible, he desired to uphold. He rallied under the banner of the Emperor against the Pope, he pitted the Crown against the Tiara. Moreover there was another difficulty in the way of Luther's entering heartily into the league. The Landgrave of Hesse and others wished to see the Swiss Protestants united with the German; but to such union Luther, from that opposition to the Zwinglian doctrines which had broken out so violently at the Marburg Conference, was most decidedly averse; perhaps the aversion abated as time rolled on, but there is no reason to believe that it was ever overcome.

Articles, intended to form the basis of the league in future, were drawn up by the theologians of the Reformation. Earnest debates and much writing went on in the upper room now occupied by the German bookseller. We can see them at their work, the fiery Luther, the mild Melancthon, the practical Bugenhagen, the learned but less illustrious Spalatin and Myconius.

Luther drafted in vigorous German a series of articles, which

HOUSE WHERE LUTHER DREW UP THE ARTICLES.

cover twenty-eight folio pages, introduced by an explanatory preface, and followed by an appendix on the papal supremacy, written afterwards by Melancthon. The first part contains concise articles upon the fundamental truths respecting the Trinity and the death of Christ, as expressed in the creed of the Church. The second part marks out four characteristic points of Protestantism—the doctrine of justification by faith, the rejection of the mass, the condemnation of monasteries, and the denial of papal supremacy. The third part relates to matters of inferior importance, respecting which learned and prudent men of different communions might agree. A MS. of this remarkable document is preserved in the library of Heidelberg, and was published at Berlin in 1817. The tone of expression adopted in speaking of the mass, which is denounced as the greatest and most horrid abomination, the chief and most audacious of all the Popish idolatries, differs from the gentle accents in which the same subject is referred to in the Confession of Augsburg. The spirit of Luther is as visible in the one symbol, as that of Melancthon in the other. We think we see signs in Melancthon's countenance of being chafed a little, as he stands by his friend's elbow, and listens to the trumpet tones in which he reads out some of his anti-Popish home truths; and it is matter of fact that when it came to signing the document, Melancthon did not add his name without some reservation. Certainly, if the Confession of Augsburg spoke peace, that of Schmalkalden breathed war.

As stated already, the League was first formed in 1531. It was renewed in 1535; but the theological articles subsequently adopted by the leaguers, and intended to anticipate and deny any new Popish symbol which might be produced, were not drawn up until the year 1537.

It was upon the 7th of February that Luther and his companions, after passing in their wintry journey through Grimma, Altenburg, and Saxe-Weimar, reached Schmalkalden. There

Luther was well taken care of—as he says, eating bread with the Landgrave, and drinking wine with the Nurembergers; but he complained, within a week after his arrival, that the business he came for proceeded too slowly. It is clear, however, that already he had drawn up the articles, and had debated upon them with his companions. No doubt they had previously been conceived and considered, and we may suppose but little remained to be done. However that might be, the second week Luther became very ill. How he was drugged at the time he broadly declares in his "Table Talk," by saying, "When I was ill at Schmalkalden, the doctors made me take medicine as though I had been a great bull." He suffered severely from an attack of the stone; it inflicted upon him excruciating torments, and made him think he should die in the town. Indeed, death seemed so near that one of the princes gave him the promise, "If, contrary to our hopes, it be the will of God to take you from us, be not concerned about your wife and children, for they shall be treated as if they were my own." Within the bedroom described—where lay the sleeping child—in all probability the Reformer endured the agony which his biographers relate; there he expected to exchange time for eternity. But at the end of a fortnight his friends resolved to remove him, and he was conveyed first to a place called Tambach, and then to Saxe-Gotha, where he experienced relief after the removal, it is said, of no less than six stones, one the size of a bean. Thence he proceeded to Erfurt, his old home; then to Weimar, where he was ever welcome; then to Altenburg, to be the guest of Spalatin; and at last to Wittenberg, which he reached in a state of extreme weakness.

One other place of interest in Schmalkalden is associated with Luther. It is the large Gothic church which stands in the market-place, near the "Crown," and which has in the choir some remarkably good pointed windows of about the fourteenth century. As I was looking at the edifice, and inquiring how I could enter, an old man, who proved to be the sexton, popped his head out of an opposite window, and hastily came downstairs to comply with my wishes.

The interior, like other German Protestant churches, is considerably disfigured by modern alterations, and there are, as usual, portraits of the two great saints of the Reformation, Martin and Philip. A curious carved wooden triptich remains fixed behind the Lutheran altar, covered with black cloth, on which stands a cross, and on each side a tall candlestick. The pulpit is old, but apparently not so old as the first half of the sixteenth century. However, the sexton would have it that it had been occupied by the Reformer. It is certain that he preached in this church at the time the League was held, and that within these walls the great men who were in Schmalkalden joined with the multitude of the towns-people, as they crowded the edifice to listen to his inspiring eloquence.[1]

Climbing up a stone staircase near one of the entrances I reached a room, the treasures of which were readily displayed. On shelves against the wall was a goodly array of volumes of divinity, including fathers and reformers; some in vellum and hog-skin bindings, almost as fresh as when they came out of the binder's hands. The sexton laid open a splendid Latin Bible, a gem of early printing—specimen of an art so perfect in its origin, that Hallam truly compares it to Minerva, springing full-armed out of the head of Jupiter. It has brilliant illuminations, in keeping with its beautiful typography. An old map of Jerusalem affixed to the wall sets geography at defiance, and completely bewilders anyone who might seek to identify some of the well-known localities of the holy city. As I was looking at it, the zealous exhibitor of church curiosities unlocked an enormous

---

[1] He says, on the 9th of February, that the day before, he addressed the princes in the parish church, which was so large and lofty, that in it his voice was like the voice of a mouse.

iron-bound chest, which might have stood there when Luther preached in the church, and forthwith brought out, and set on the table, four large silver tankards, four large silver cups, two great candlesticks, and two boxes filled with wafers, such as are still used in Lutheran churches for the holy communion. "There," said he, pointing to two cups smaller than the others, and decked with precious stones, "Luther used them in celebrating the eucharist."

When I had completed my examination of the relics and of the church, my attention was arrested by pleasant voices united in singing hymns, the sound of which issued from the windows of a large building, under the shadow of the Stadt Kirche. It was the schoolhouse, which so frequently appears in Germany close by the house of God, in accordance with Lutheran laws and traditions. That summer morning, when nature was so quiet and the town so still, and the architecture looked so quaint and carried one back so far into the past, there was a poetical witchery in those murmuring tones of schoolboy songsters. But presently came the outrush of the youngsters, and the clattering of their feet on the stone steps, and the prattle and laughter of their merry lips, which, if it dispelled all moody sentimentalism, woke one up to the cheerful realities of German life, and to the consciousness that the hour was come for the mid-day meal.

XVII.

HALLE, IN SAXONY.

HALLE contains one of the great railway junctions in the north of Germany. It is a place of immense traffic, owing to its central position, and possesses several important manufactories; but its chief commercial boast rests on the salt springs of the neighbourhood, which some time since produced nearly 500,000 bushels a year. The name of the town is supposed to be derived from a Greek word signifying salt.

The history of Halle runs back to an early date. The Moritz Kirche, in the lower part of the town, near the saltworks, has a choir belonging to the fourteenth century, and it began to be built in the middle of the twelfth. But the chief historical interest of Halle arises from its university, from its orphan-house, and from incidents connected with the Lutheran Reformation. The university in its present form was founded as late as 1815, when the University of Wittenberg became incorporated with it; but it existed before in a separate capacity, having originated in 1694, under the auspices of

Frederick I. of Prussia, to be dissolved under the dictatorship of the first Napoleon. The Pietist influences which created this seminary have fashioned its character throughout its varying fortunes. It has generally been identified with the study of evangelical theology, and until of late retained amongst its ornaments the distinguished Professor Tholuck. The Pietist influence manifest in the institution of the university is further manifest in the history of the well-known orphan-house, commenced by A. H. Franke in 1698. That eminent divine, fired by an unwonted charity towards the poor and destitute, established schools for the education of children of both sexes, and trusted their support to Divine Providence, much after the manner renewed at Bristol by Mr. Müller in his orphan establishment. Historical associations connected with the Reformation cluster around the churches, and around what remains of the palace of the Archbishop of Magdeburg. In that palace, it may be noticed, the humiliating act of submission was performed by Philip, Landgrave of Hesse, at the feet of Charles V., after the defeat, in 1547, of the Protestant army at Mühlberg.

In the university, the orphan-house, and the story of Philip linked to the old archiepiscopal residence, are traces of the potent influence of Martin Luther; and it is in keeping with the place he occupied in relation to the great town of Germany, and to Halle especially, that high up against the triforium of the Markt Kirche, has been fixed a terra-cotta medallion, with the inscription, " *Sanctus Doctor M. Lutherus, propheta Germaniæ.*"

I visited Halle simply with the expectation of seeing a town which Luther must often have seen, and found it by no means attractive until I came upon the market-place.

The market-place certainly is worth seeing—a large square, lined with antiquated houses and shops—presenting an agreeable picture to the eyes of an archæologist. The gaunt red tower stands isolated, and near it is the Markt Kirche—where appears

MARKET-PLACE, HALLE.

the Reformer's medallion,—a fine Gothic edifice of the sixteenth century, flanked by four towers, two of which are united by a bridge, and together form the habitation of the keeper of the church. Within is an altar-piece by Hübner. There are also pictures by Lucas Cranach, Luther's friend.

As I was standing with my companion and looking up to the church towers, our attention was directed to a little shop window, displaying books and photographs. We stepped in and selected some capital views of Halle; and upon informing the bookseller of our interest in the Saxon reformer, he proceeded to say, that very near stood a house, in which our hero lodged when passing through the town. Having mastered the information conveyed, we repaired to the *Scheemer Strasse*, and pacing down a narrow dirty street, lighted on a shop, now modernized, with the following inscription on the wall :—

"Here in the hostelry of the Golden Lock (Schlosschen) lodged Dr. Martin Luther in the beginning of August, 1545."

Over the doorway next the shop is an ogive arch, with a pinnacle ornament on each side of it, and two heads underneath, and what looks like a lock in the middle. According to one of the meanings of the word *schlosschen*, a lock was the sign of the hostelry.

Here, then, we had found a house in which Luther had lodged the last autumn of his life, the fall of the year 1545, a little more than five months before he left the world. It appears that he became tired of Wittenberg towards the end of his days, being dissatisfied with the state of things in the university as well as in the town; and I thought while looking at the old doorway under the ogive arch, that probably he had come hither that August to find some relief from his troubles.

On returning home I turned over the fifth volume of De Wette's "*Briefe*" of Luther, hoping to find there a letter belonging to the month of August, and dated Halle. Such a letter there is not but under date 19th August, 1545, there is a letter from Wittenberg to his friend Amsdorf, with this passage at the commencement,—" Grace and peace in the Lord. At last I came home, reverend father in Christ, on the 18th of August, suffering from the disease of the stone. Nor am I to-day altogether free from pain. Although not so much distressed as yesterday, nevertheless I labour under an intolerable thirst. But enough of this." And then he proceeds to notice something which he had heard at Leipzig. From this letter it is plain that he had returned to Wittenberg after the middle of August, and that he had recently visited Leipzig. His biographers state that he left Wittenberg in May, and that he visited Merseburg and Zeitz, as well as Leipzig. There is a letter written to his wife in the month of July, dated Leipzig, in which he speaks of the wickedness of Wittenberg, and declares his intention to leave it. Indeed, he gives directions for the sale of his property in the town.

Leipzig and Halle are very near each other. It quite comports with the letters to believe the tradition inscribed over the doorway in the *Scheemer Strasse*, that Luther made some stay in Halle in the early part of August; and it confers a touching interest on the dwelling to think of it as having been the scene of one of those fits of the stone, from which he suffered so severely in the Sannersche Haus at Schmalkalden. I applied for permission to enter and see any room which tradition might have connected with the Reformer, but learned that there was nothing in the interior identified with his memory, and that the apartments had been adapted to domestic convenience.

A characteristic letter written by him, at a later date, from Halle, is well known; and it is not unlikely that this guest-house of the Golden Lock having been Luther's resting-place on a former visit, would be so at another time. Possibly, then, the letter I am about to introduce was written within those very walls.

He had left Wittenberg and his beloved Kate, and was on his

way to Eisleben with his sons, to settle a quarrel in the Mansfeld family. Pausing at Halle he wrote in this facetious style:

"Grace and peace in the Lord. Beloved Katie, to-day at half-past eight o'clock we have come to Halle, but have not reached Eisleben. For a great Anabaptist, with water-floods and ice-blocks has covered the land and threatened us with a rebaptism. We could not get back on account of the river Mulda. Therefore we remain quiet at Halle, between the two streams. Not that we want to drink water, for we get good Torgau beer and Rhine wine, and with it refresh and comfort ourselves. Should the river Saale rage again, we, our servants, and the ferryman would not tempt God, by going on the river any more, for the devil is furious, and dwells in the water. It is better to keep out of his way than to complain; nor need we become the jest of the Pope and his people. I should not have believed that the Saale could have made such a brewing, breaking over the causeway with such a rattling noise. But no more of this; pray for us and be godly. I hold that if thou hadst been here, what thou wouldst have advised is just the thing which we have done. Herewith I commit thee to God. Amen. At Halle, on the Conversion of St. Paul, anno 1546."

Luther never visited the hotel of the Lock after that—never saw Halle again. He went to Eisleben to die. The next time he passed through the town of the salt springs was in his coffin.

XVIII.

WITTENBERG.

WITTENBERG takes its name from the white sand-hills rising in its neighbourhood, amidst a plain cut by the river Elbe; on its northern bank stands this cradle of the Reformation — this Protestant Mecca. There is a striking contrast between the Elbe, as it sweeps through the charming scenes of Saxon Switzerland, and as it flows through this flat district to the north, the picturesque rocks and the abounding foliage of the upper region of the river making the willows and oak shrubs which fringe the lower part appear the more uninteresting and dreary. The town contains about 11,000 inhabitants, and is a long straggling place, one wide street running from end to end, paralleled and intersected by others, where may be seen a few interesting specimens of domestic architecture, and some public edifices of rather an imposing kind.

I reached the town with my daughter in the summer of 1872, on the anniversary of the battle of Sedan; and along the road was reminded ever and anon, by waving flags and military displays, of the great German victory of 1870. On leaving the railway station and walking down the long street we found the people absorbed in the celebration of the event which had so increased the power and glory of the Fatherland—an event clearly running on the same line of divine Providence as the disposition of affairs in the sixteenth century, when the monstrous pretensions of the Roman Papacy received a fatal blow; for the policy of Prince Bismarck is a political corollary drawn after the lapse of three centuries, from the ecclesiastical reforms of Martin Luther.

Martin Luther came to Wittenberg in the autumn of 1508. The town then contained three hundred and fifty-six houses, and about two thousand inhabitants; none of the houses very stately, none of the inhabitants very rich. Military occupations and sensual pleasures are said to have been at that time characteristics of the place, intermingled with fondness for the exhibition of religious plays. Payments for fire-arms, for races, for oxen given as prizes, for paintings and masks, for scaffolding, and for dresses in connection with the Passion-week plays, figure prominently in the municipal accounts during some years before Luther's arrival. Afterwards beer must have been most abundant in Wittenberg, for it numbered no less than one hundred and seventy-two breweries! and it was a saying that in the burghers' houses "the cuckoo could be heard on winter evenings," so frequent were the notes issuing from the necks of well-filled ale-bottles.

The university had come into existence only six years before Luther's arrival. English universities are of slow growth and of permanent duration. Oxford and Cambridge struggled with difficulties ere they attained established power; and the story of Durham and London seems, in this respect, somewhat like that of their much older and stronger sisters: but German universities rapidly rise and suddenly change. Erfurt and Wittenberg both disappeared about the same time; the former being wholly suppressed in 1816, the latter being incorporated with Halle the year before. Wittenberg shot up at once into importance: one hundred and seventy-nine students entered in 1508. Altogether then there might be about four or five hundred; in a few years the number increased to two thousand. It was less under ecclesiastical control than Louvain, Cologne, and Leipzig, being protected neither by Pope nor bishop, but by the Elector,—a circumstance which proved favourable to Luther's proceedings. The students must have been an unruly set, and by no means reverential as to episcopal dignity; for a rector was assassinated by one who had been expelled; Melancthon narrowly escaped with his life from the hands of a pupil; and the Bishop of Brandenburg was so insulted in the person of his officers, that he laid the town under interdict, and made the people pay a fine of two thousand guldens.

The situation of Wittenberg was not attractive. The flat plain around the town presented a contrast to the scenery Luther had left; the banks of the Elbe being very different from the Golden Mead near Erfurt, and the grassy slopes around his beloved Eisenach. His distaste for the place frequently appeared, and he expressed his wonder that any one should have thought of founding a university in such a situation.

But here he was destined to spend the greater portion of his life. Hence Wittenberg, beyond every other place, presents points of contact with his history, and will therefore the longer detain our attention.

I. Luther at Home in Wittenberg.

In a building near the Elster Gate, at the eastern extremity of the town, he took up his abode first as a monk, then as a professor. Originally an Augustinian monastery, it was afterwards devoted to college purposes. As the Reformation proceeded, one after another of the monks abandoned their cells; and at length the prior gave up the building into the hands of the Elector, who converted it entirely into a university establishment.

A portion of it connected with Martin Luther remains still, and of course attracts the attention of every visitor to Wittenberg. As the railway station lies not far from the Elster Gate, you soon see the venerable edifice, the gable end peering out as you pass into the town; but we had to walk nearly to the extreme end of it on the side opposite, before we could discover the person who had the key to Luther's rooms.

THE AUGUSTINIAN MONASTERY, WITTENBERG.

Entering the courtyard under a gateway, we found ourselves in front of a long range of building, with no architectural pretensions, but recently renovated, and presenting a heavy-walled, old, monastic-looking house, dotted with several windows, and capped by a high roof. The woman who acted as cicerone took us up a staircase; and on the first floor we were ushered into a good-sized room, of dark panelling, and windows looking out into the courtyard. A large German stove, covered with singular devices, stood on the side opposite to the window; and that, we were informed, was Luther's stove, made and decorated according to his own design. Near the window stood a chair and table at which he wrote; and over a door leading into a second apartment belonging to the Reformer may be seen the autograph in chalk of the Russian emperor, Peter the Great. A jug is shown from which Luther drank his beer, and a curious cast of his face taken after his death. Besides these there are two portraits of him painted by Cranach, and amongst the Protestant relics is his professorial chair.

Let us tarry in this room before we visit other spots.

Motley, in his "United Netherlands," has sketched a vivid picture of Philip II. at his writing-table: his grey head whitening fast at sixty years of age, his frame slight, his digestion weak, his manners more glacial and sepulchral than ever; working as hard as a slave, scrawling his "apostilles," stretching innumerable threads across the surface of Christendom—covering it with a net converged in that silent cell,—the whole meant to sweep Protestantism out of the Netherlands, and to restore Popish influence over England. In contrast with this, think of the Saxon monk in his Wittenberg chamber, also seated at a writing-table, in the vigour of his manhood, with burly frame, strong digestion, and genial soul; his outbursts of humour lighting up that broad honest face of his with sunny daylight. He studies hard the Bible and St. Augustine, and muses much upon views of truth opening on his soul, and then writes comment after comment, lecture after lecture, sermon after sermon, letter after letter—all bearing on a design the opposite of the Spanish monarch; for he seeks to liberate, not enthral; to push on the progress of the ages, not to crush them back. And with what different results do the two workers ply their tools! How Philip's webs are scattered to the winds! How Luther's work endures to this day, and inspires other workers who follow in the same track!

Seated in that old chair, bending over that old table, Luther prepared for lecturing to his students. He did not like going over old Aristotelian ground; notwithstanding he obeyed the call of duty.

LUTHER'S STUDY AT WITTENBERG.

"But now, at God's command," he writes, on the 17th of March, 1509, "or by His permission, I am here in Wittenberg. If you desire to know my condition, I would say it is, by God's favour, very good ; saving that I must force myself to study philosophy, which from the beginning I have wished to relinquish for theology —that theology which seeks after the inside of the nut, the kernel of the wheat beneath the husk, the marrow within the bone. But God is God, and man often—nay, always—erreth in his judgment. This is our God, and He shall guide us in His lovingkindness for ever."

One cannot help thinking, in connection with these rooms, of the oft-told anecdote how, when employed in studying the 22nd Psalm, Luther shut himself up with a little bread and salt for three days and three nights, gave no answer to those who knocked at the door, and on its being forcibly opened appeared sitting at his writing-table as one in a dream. In reference to the power of abstinence he thus manifested Melancthon remarks, "I have observed him for four following days, when he was in perfect health, neither to eat nor drink anything."

The translation of the Scriptures, commenced at the Wartburg, was completed and perfected at Wittenberg. From the beginning of the work he had devoted much time to the study of the original languages. In that study he persevered from year to year after returning from exile, and was no doubt assisted by the eminent scholars connected with the university. In S. Winkworth's edition of Kœnig's illustrated "Life of Luther" there is an engraving of the Reformer seated on a chair, pen in hand, consulting his friend, who, leaning on his shoulder with an open book in one hand, is seen engaged in some explanations ; and this picture is as true as it is pleasant.

The New Testament was finished in 1522. The complete Bible did not appear until 1534. After that it underwent revision. Turning again to Kœnig's volume, we see another picture, representing Luther, surrounded by a number of the German Reformers, consulting together on the subject. Luther stands between Melancthon and Bugenhagen. On the left Jonas is looking up towards Luther, while on the right Kreuziger is seen in conversation with the Rabbis. The picture embodies the following abridged statement from Mathesius:

"When the whole Bible had been published in German, Dr. Luther takes it up again from the beginning with much earnestness, diligence, and prayer, and convokes, as it were, a Sanhedrim of the best men that could be found, who come together every week at his house—Dr. Bugenhagen, Dr. Jonas, Dr. Kreuziger, Master Melancthon, M. Aurogallus, with G. Rörer, the corrector, and often some foreign doctors and scholars. Now when our Doctor had looked through the Bible already published, and besides inquired among the Jews and foreign linguists, and picked up good words by asking old Germans, he came into the assembly with his old Latin and new German Bible, and always brought a Hebrew text also. Melancthon brought the Greek text, Dr. Kreuziger the Hebrew and Chaldee, and the professors had their Rabbis with them. Each had prepared himself beforehand for the passage on which they were to deliberate, and looked at the commentators thereon. After due exhortation each stated his opinion, which he proved to the best of his ability by the grammar or context, or testimony of the learned, till at length in the year 1542 this work was, by God's grace, accomplished." Bugenhagen afterwards kept up an annual celebration of the completion of the task, by inviting a select party of learned friends to what was commonly called *the Festival of the Translation of the Scriptures*.[1]

Luther's version has won the highest praise. " Idiomatic, vital in every part, clothed in the racy language of common life, it created, apart from its religious influence, an epoch in the literary development of the German nation." To this accurate estimate,

---

[1] Adam, "Vit. Germ. Theologorum," p. 318, in "Vita Joan Bugenhagii."

formed by a Protestant American critic, I would add the glowing eulogium of a Catholic German scholar, one who himself seeks to reform the Church to which he belongs. Speaking of Luther's writings in general, as well as his translation, Dr. Döllinger observes, " It was Luther's overpowering greatness of mind and marvellous many-sidedness which made him to be the man of his time and of his people ; and it is correct to say that there never has been a German who has so intuitively understood his people, and in turn has been by the nation so perfectly comprehended, I might say absorbed by it, as this Augustinian monk at Wittenberg.

" Heart and mind of the Germans were in his hand like the lyre in the hand of the musician. Moreover he has given to his people more than any other man in Christian ages has ever given to a people—language, manual for popular instruction, Bible, hymns of worship ; and everything which his opponents, in their turn, had to offer or to place in comparison with these, showed itself tame, powerless, and colourless by the side of his sweeping eloquence. They stammered, he spoke with the tongue of an orator ; it is he only who has stamped the imperishable seal of his own soul alike upon the German language, and upon the German mind ; and even those Germans who abhorred him as the powerful heretic and seducer of the nation, cannot escape ; they must discourse with his words, they must think with his thoughts."[1]

It is highly probable that in the room described Luther received another eminent translator of the Scriptures, William Tyndale. Friends and enemies contemporary with the latter have mentioned a visit by him to Wittenberg as a well-known circumstance, corroborated in some degree by Mathesius, who, as we have seen, speaks of assistance afforded by "foreign doctors and scholars." And now the statement as to Tyndale, questioned by many, seems to be fully established by Mr. Demaus and Mr. Arber. History

---

[1] Döllinger, " Vorträge," etc., Munich, 1872. Fisher on the Reformation, pp. 112, 163.

preserves no record of the conversation between the German and English Reformers; but many will linger, in fancy, over their meeting as far more interesting than the interview so much talked about of Henry VIII. and Francis I. on the Field of the Cloth of Gold. Tyndale, though a competent scholar, and really an original translator from the Hebrew and Greek, made much use of Luther's version. On comparing the folio of Luther's Testament printed in 1522 with the quarto of Tyndale printed 1525, the resemblance is striking. The general appearance of the page is the same, the arrangement of the texts is the same, and the appropriation of the margins is also the same. And still further, what is of far more importance, although it is now for the first time indicated, the marginal notes, those "pestilent glosses," against which the indignation of the clergy was especially excited, have been to a large extent translated by Tyndale from those of Luther.[1]

In this Augustinian convent Luther, by God's help, gradually made himself what he ultimately became; and step by step we can here trace his progress along the path of his arduous enterprise.

Hither he returned from Rome with recollections which he turned into weapons of war when fighting against papal tyranny and corruption. Here he prepared for Leipzig and Worms. Up this winding staircase he came on his return from the Wartburg to sit down again in the familiar chair. Business connected with Augsburg Diets and other matters had to be arranged in this university home; and often the burden which the strong man had to carry proved more than he could bear.

Just by, outside the Elster Gate, there grows a young oak, planted on the spot where Luther burnt the Pope's Bull in December, 1520. The gable end of the monastic building may be seen rising above the town walls, and from one of the upper windows the smoke of the famous conflagration might have been

[1] "William Tyndale, a Biography," p. 129. Arber's "First printed New Testament," p. 67.

watched curling up to heaven. In this conventual abode Luther determined to do the daring deed, and walked through the gateway opposite the chamber to the spot where he cast into the flames a pile of documents regarded with superstitious reverence by many who saw them crackling in the flames. At that hour he crossed the Rubicon of the Reformation, pulled down the bridge which cut off retreat, burnt every boat for escape, and rendered reconciliation with Rome impossible. It required no small effort to perform such an act ; and he must have come back to his chamber wondering whereunto all this would grow. Here he recorded the simple fact in the following lines :

"A.D. 1520, 10th of December, at the hour of nine, were burnt at Wittenberg, by the Elster Gate, near the Holy Cross, all the books of the Pope, the rescripts, the decretals of Clement VI., the extravagants, the new Bull of Leo X., the *Summa Angelica*, the *Chrysposus* of Eck, and other works of his and of Emser, in order that incendiary papists may see that it requires no great power to burn books they cannot answer. This is a new thing." It was so as it regards Bulls, not as it regards Protestant books ; there was, therefore, a grim, satirical retaliation in reducing to ashes these authoritative documents.

In another place he says, " If any one ask why I act thus, I will answer him that it is an old custom to burn bad books. The apostles burnt books to the value of 5,000 deniers."

Luther, like Paul, might have enumerated amongst his responsibilities, "that which cometh upon me daily, the care of the churches." We find him saying, " I am every day so overwhelmed with letters, that my table, benches, footstools, desks, windows, cases, boards, and everything are full of letters, inquiries, causes, complaints, petitions, etc. On me falleth the whole weight of the Church and State, as neither the ecclesiastics nor magistrates perform their duties." Again, with a touch of humour, he remarks, " I need have two secretaries to keep up my correspondence ; pity my unhappy fortune. I am conventual preacher, table reader, director of studies. I am vicar, or in words, eleven priors in one, conservator of Litzkau, pleader and assessor at Torgau, Paulinic reader and commentator on the psalms;—add to all these the assaults of the world, the flesh, and the devil."

We may add that his labours as author and editor were something prodigious. "It has been calculated," says Hardwick, in his "Manual on the Reformation," "that in one year as many as one hundred and eighty-three books were published in his name." To that year belong the first Lutheran hymns, which produced an immense effect. It is wonderful the amount of work he accomplished in the course of his life, and it is curious to notice how he thus practically demonstrated the power and efficacy of the human will at the time when he was engaged in laborious attempts to prove theoretically its impotence and bondage.

In the summer of 1525 Luther entered the married life. He wedded Catherine von Bora, a nun, who, like himself, had renounced communion with Rome; and in her society he found a comfort and solace amidst his labours and trials. Kate made Martin a good wife, Martin made Kate a good husband; and their pure Christian domestic life practically confuted the superstitious sophisms of Romish celibacy. Weddings in Germany are followed by festivals, when the bride is conducted to her new home; and from the account we have of the feast after Luther's wedding we get an amusing insight into the difficulties besetting his change of life.[1]

[1] Some say she was not attractive in appearance, and certain portraits to be seen in Germany might confirm that notion; but other portraits, when carefully examined, suggest a different idea, and make me think she must have been a pleasant-looking person. I have just discovered a passage in the "Venetian Correspondence,' which supports the favourable view. Francesco Contarini, writing on the 2nd of November, 1535, describes his visit to Wittenberg, and an interview he had with Agricola, Spalatin, and others. He observes that Luther "remained at home with his wife, who was a nun, and, according to their account, a very handsome and virtuous young woman."—" State Papers."

LUTHER'S WIFE: KATHARINA VON BORA AS A BRIDE.

"The apartment known as Luther's dwelling in the Augustinian cloister," remarks Dr. Sears, "was undoubtedly the scene of this solemnity. Seven of the invitations sent to different individuals have been preserved, and give us a view of the peculiar and somewhat awkward position of Luther, as well as a picture of the times.

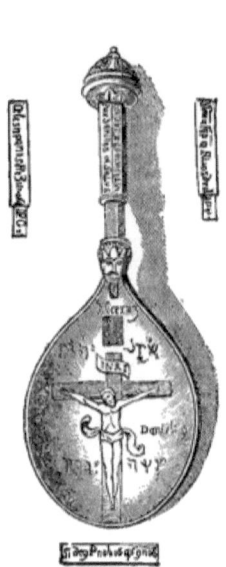

LUTHER'S EATING-SPOON, USED WHEN TRAVELLING, AFTERWARDS GIVEN BY HIM TO CASPAR AQUILA.

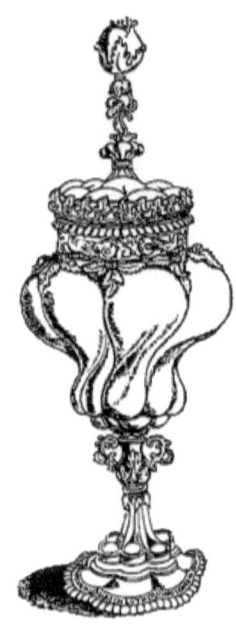

BRIDAL CUP GIVEN TO LUTHER BY THE UNIVERSITY OF WITTENBERG.

"The first is that written to Chancellor Rühel, Luther's brother-in-law, and two other Mansfeld court officers, and reads as follows: 'According to the wish of my dear father, I have taken me a wife; and on account of evil speakers, and that no hindrance might be placed in the way, I have hastened the act. It is my wish that the festive occasion of bringing my bride home take place a week from next Tuesday, and that I may enjoy your presence and receive your blessing. Since these are times of commotion [the insurrection of the peasants] and danger, I cannot urge your attendance: but if you have a desire to come, and can do so, and bring with you my dear father and mother, you can easily understand that it would give me great joy; and whatever

LUTHER'S BETROTHAL RING.

[presents] you may receive from good friends for my poverty will be very welcome.' Another invitation, sent to Dolzig, the Elector's Marshal, is written with characteristic humour. 'No doubt,' he says, 'the strange rumour hath reached you that I have

ENLARGED SKETCH OF ORNAMENTATION ON THE BETROTHAL RING.
(ANTE-REFORMATION STYLE.)

become a husband. Though this is a very singular affair, which I myself can scarcely believe, nevertheless the witnesses are so numerous that I am bound in honour to believe it; and I have concluded to have a collation next Tuesday for my father and mother, and other good friends, to seal the same and make it sure. I therefore beg you, if it is not too much trouble, to provide venison for me, and be present yourself to help affix the seal with becoming joy.' At this time the city presented to Luther several casks of beer; and the university gave a large silver tankard, plated with gold on the outside and inside, weighing five pounds and a quarter. It was purchased, in the year 1800, from the heirs, by the University of Greifswald, for one hundred rix-dollars."[1]

LUTHER'S WEDDING-RING, WITH INSCRIPTION, "WHAT GOD HATH JOINED TOGETHER," ETC.

There is a double window-seat in the room of the old convent. It is raised above the floor, and there is just space enough for two people to rest opposite one another, and to look out through the diamond panes upon the court below. Here, we are told, Dr. Luther and his spouse would sit *tête-à-tête*, and catch the warm rays of the sun, and inhale the fragrance of flowers on the window-sill, and watch the evening shadows gathering over tower and turret, and the stars sparkling in the sky overhead, and the moon walking in her brightness. For all these natural charms the Reformer had a heart as sensitive as any man; and if Kate was more prosaic, her love for good Dr. Martin would make up for any want of intellectual sympathy, and would enable her to find music in all his utterances.

Here, of course, as children were born and nursed, and as they grew up, family joys beat in the hearts of father and mother. Every

[1] "Luther," by Sears, p. 329.

reader is familiar with Luther's Christmas-tree, and imagination easily reproduces it, with its tiny lights, and pretty decorations, and simple presents; Luther singing a carol, accompanied by his own lute; the children playing on the floor; Kate sitting demurely in one corner, and the servant-maid in the other; whilst Philip Melancthon, as a visitor, leans over a chair and listens to his friend.

This room, so rich in memories, was darkened by troubles in the summer and autumn of the year 1527, when the plague entered Wittenberg and alarmed the inhabitants. The students of the university fled to Jena; only Luther and Pomeranus, attended by chaplains, remained at their post. The Reformer resisted the exhortations and entreaties of the Elector to depart, and in letters to Spalatin maintained that the danger of contagion was exaggerated by the popular panic. However, before the year's end, we learn from his letters that sickness had entered his dwelling. He writes, Nov. 10, 1527, "My little favourite John does not salute thee, because he is too ill, but he asks your prayer on his behalf. For the last twelve days he has taken nothing but liquids. Now he begins to eat a little. It is wonderful to see how the child keeps up his spirits: he would be as merry as ever if it were not for his extreme debility. Margaret Mochine's gathering was lanced yesterday, and she is beginning to be better already. I have put her into our winter bedroom; we are in our great front room, Jenny in the chamber with the stove, and Augustine's wife in her own apartment."

Laying down this letter, which so plainly identifies the rooms at Wittenberg, and peoples them with their respective occupants, we take up another, dated the 31st of December the same year: "My little son was all but dead, but he has recovered again. . . . It has pleased God to give me a daughter. . . . We are all well except myself; though sound in body and shut out from the world, I suffer within from the devil and his angels."

Seven months later, August 5, 1528, comes the touching record

"My little daughter Elizabeth is dead. It is wonderful how sick at heart this loss has left me. I feel like a woman, I am so affected by this calamity. I could not have believed that parental affection could have been so drawn out towards a child."

Amidst these troubles he thought he was dying himself, and declared death would be welcome, though he was ready to live, he said, for the sake of spreading the gospel and comforting the faint-hearted.

Several years afterwards—in 1542—his daughter Magdalene died at the age of thirteen. Kneeling by her bedside, the father prayed, "I love her dearly, but as it is Thy will, gracious God, to take her hence, I will gladly surrender her that she may be with Thee." "Magdalene, my child," he exclaimed, as he bent over her in her last moments, "you would be glad to remain here with your father: are you willing to depart and go to that other Father?"

"Yes," she replied, "just as God wills." Hiding his tears, he said, "If the flesh be so strong, how will it be with the spirit? Well, whether we live or die, we are the Lord's."

She died folded in his arms. When she had been placed in her coffin, he exclaimed, "How well it is with you! Ah, dear Lene, you will rise again and shine like a star—yea, as the sun."

But this same room, on which again and again fell the shadow of death, also brightened with the purest sunlight of domestic joy. Did not an example of this occur when the now famous letter came from Coburg to his eldest son, then four years old? It was written the 19th of June, 1530:

"Grace and peace in Christ, my darling little son. I am glad that you study and pray diligently. Go on, my Jonny; and when I come home I will bring some beautiful things for you. I know of a pleasant garden, where many children go, and wear little golden coats, and gather from the trees fine apples and pears, and cherries and plums; they sing and play, and are happy; they have pretty little horses, with golden bits and silver saddles. I asked the master of the garden whose children these were. He said, 'They are children who love to pray and learn, and are good.' I then said, 'Dear sir, I too have a son, named Jonny Luther. May he not also come into the garden, that he too may eat these beautiful apples and pears, and ride on these fine horses, and play with the children?' The man said, 'If he loves to pray and learn, and is good, he shall come into the garden, and Philip and Justus too;' and when they are all come together, they shall have fifes and drums and lutes, and all kinds of music, and dance, and shoot with little crossbows. And he showed me a fine grass plat in the garden for dancing: and there were hanging over it golden fifes and drums, and fine silver crossbows. But it was early, and the children had not yet eaten; so as I could not wait for their dancing, I said to the man, 'My dear sir, I will hasten away and write all about this to my dear little Jonny, that he may pray and study and be good, so that he may come into this garden. He has an Aunt Lene, and she must come too.' The man said, 'That is right; go and tell him so.' Therefore, my dear little Jonny, learn and pray well; and tell Philip and Justus to learn and pray, so that you may all come together into the garden. And now I commend you to God. Greet Aunt Lene, and give her a kiss for me.—Your dear father, MARTIN LUTHER."

Sunny influences were often shed over the university home, and we see him " seated at table amidst his grave-visaged friends and disciples, his children playing beside him or walking with him in his garden on the margin of the little pond in the grounds of that sombre monastery, once sacred to celibacy, and now become the abode of the married Luther and his family. We hear him meditating aloud, and finding in all that he looked upon, the flowers, the fruits, the birds flying over his head or singing in the trees, topics for grave and pious thoughts." [2]

---

[1] Philip was Melancthon's son; Justus, the son of Justus Jonas.   [2] Michelet.

Luther's two rooms in the convent betoken nothing like grandeur. Though the intimate friend of nobles and princes, sometimes even entertaining them at his table, he must have lived in great simplicity. Indeed, it is notorious that at one period he was very poor, and found it hard work to make ends meet. He applied himself to the arts of wood-turning, clock-making, and gardening, with a view to the increase of his small income. He complained that he got into debt. When asked for eight florins, he replied with another question, "Where on earth am I to get them?" He was very charitable and very hospitable, and expended, he says, five hundred gulden in the kitchen, to say nothing of clothing, ornaments, and almsgiving, when his income did not reach above two hundred. He pawned three goblets, presents from friends, for fifty florins, and sold one for twelve. He received next to nothing for his publications, and was glad of provisions sent by friends. It was plain that he was no skilful economist, no good manager; but I do not gather from what he says in some of his letters that he was always in straitened circumstances. There can be no question about his being through the chief part of his life a poor man; but towards the end his condition improved, as presents of land were made to him by the Elector John of Saxony; and his property when he died amounted to about nine thousand gulden.

Luther's love of music is known; and in this Wittenberg chamber he loved to sing, and play, and compose music; but one is sorry to find that Dr. Sears, who has carefully examined the Reformer's history, believes there is no evidence of his being, as is generally supposed, the author of the tune known as the Old Hundredth. But a friend of Luther tells how he spent many a happy hour in singing with him; how he had seen the dear man so happy and joyful that he could neither be tired nor satisfied; how he conversed on musical subjects; how he composed tunes for the celebration of the Lord's Supper, and kept him three weeks together at Wittenberg, writing notes for service in the parish church. Luther married music to theology, and thought religion never more beautiful than when in company with the daughters of song.

Luther had great conversational power, and was to reformed divines, with whom he mingled, as much of a colloquial oracle as was ever Dr. Johnson to the wits and literati of London. But instead of one Boswell, the German Reformer had several, and each, intent on his vocation, jotted down his words with the utmost reverence and affection. "They were," says Hazlitt, "with him at his uprising and his down-lying; they looked over his shoulder as he read or wrote his letters: did he utter an exclamation of pain or of pleasure, of joy or of sorrow, down it went; did he aspirate a thought above breath, it was caught by the intent ear of one or other of the listeners, and committed to paper." Luther knew this, and it much amused him. Once he saw a disciple hard at work with pencil and paper; when, slily filling his wooden spoon with gruel, he threw it into the face of the reporter, bidding him "put that down." Luther could have been no phlegmatic German, according to the common notion formed of his countrymen by English people; for his conversation sparkled with humour and overflowed with emotion, while it revealed depths of spiritual wisdom and practical sagacity, of religious experience and of theological thought.

It must have been a rare privilege to sit with him in his Wittenberg chamber and hear him talk; and next to the advantage of having listened to his voice is the benefit of perusing the pages of his "Tischreden." A translation of it was printed a few years ago in Bohn's Standard Library, under the title of "Table Talk;" and the history of the book is very curious. Nearly all the copies of the original work were destroyed by order of Gregory XIII.; but in 1626, a gentleman, in digging a foundation for a new house, discovered a book carefully wrapped in coarse linen cloth and covered with beeswax, which proved to be the lost production. This gentleman sent it to a Captain Bell, who translated and published it, being stimulated to do so by a strange dream. When it was finished Archbishop Laud borrowed, read, and praised it, and the English House of Commons sanctioned its publication. All this we learn from Bell himself in his preface to the translation; and how remarkable it is to find Anglo-Catholic and Puritan doing honour to the record of the Reformer's conversation!

II. Luther with his Friends.

There never was a man more thoroughly independent than Luther. It is difficult for us in this age of free utterance, when it requires but little force of individuality to express any opinions whatever, to appreciate the power of standing alone, and of defying opposition such as was manifested by this sturdy Saxon. He stood up alone, or almost alone, on different occasions to protest against what was accepted by the whole, or almost the whole, of Europe. He reminds us of *Athanasius contra mundum*. But men of that order are apt to be anti-social. Isolated in their position, self-contained, as a necessary qualification for their work, and self-absorbed as a common consequence of their circumstances, they care little for the love of others, and do not crave for sympathies which are denied to them. Luther's nature was of a different cast; he was as much distinguished by the cultivation of friendship as by the assertion of independence. There never was a man who desired more to live in the love of others, or who more fondly cherished the love of others in his own life. The life of Martin Luther is so entwined with the life of Martin Luther's friends, that you cannot separate them. Staupitz, Pomeranus, Spalatin, Agricola, Justus Jonas, Melancthon, Cranach, the Electors of Saxony, and other names, occur in his memoirs and correspondence, so as to show how genial was his disposition—how highly he prized the affections of his fellow-men, how deeply he felt their desertion or neglect, how warmly he responded to the expressions of their attachment, and how he was helped by their sympathy, and the confidence he had in their intercessions with the Father of all.

Wittenberg was the scene of his closest intimacies—of some of the striking anecdotes of his social life—of most of the conversations recorded in his well-known "Table Talk."

I propose to visit three spots to find Luther in company with his friends,—the professor's house, the artist's studio, and the Elector's castle.

1. The friendship between Martin Luther and Philip Melancthon stands out most conspicuously in the story of his life, and is one of those beautiful instances of mutual confidence and affection such as in the case of Basil and Gregory, Hammond and Sanderson, not to mention more, which meet us pleasantly amidst dark surroundings of theological and ecclesiastical strife.

When my daughter and I were at Wittenberg, walking from the Augustine convent, where Luther lived, to the church at the opposite end of the town, where he lies buried, we passed the house pointed out as the residence of Melancthon. We applied for admission, which was readily granted, and were shown up a staircase which led to an apartment where it is said Melancthon studied, and conversed, and died. A table, if I remember rightly, and other relics of the great Protestant scholar, were pointed out; and on the wall hung his likeness, taken after death, the counterpart of a picture we afterwards noticed in the Dresden Gallery. Under the likeness is the following inscription, in Latin: "From this mortal life to the eternal God, and the society of the saints, he holily and placidly departed, in the sixty-third year of his age." His last words were, "No one shall pluck My sheep out of My hands." The room, now unfurnished and bare, was once filled with books and papers, as the occupant wrote his lectures, comments, documents for public use, and letters to his numerous friends. We could see him as represented in portraits, with marked features, expressive eyes, prominent nose, thin lips, capacious forehead, rough hair, and rough beard; with a loose fur-trimmed coat, almost touching his ankles; with a strange amount of neck-gear, which seems as if he wore a metal frill indescribably twisted down his bosom; with large, heavy, misshapen boots; and with a hat in one hand and a little book in the other. His wife, too, appeared, for he was married and had a family; and we fancied the worthy couple giving a genuine, hearty welcome to neighbour Martin, as he strode up the staircase and entered the room, and bestowed a double kiss, in German fashion, on the university professor. Here they would confer together touching important matters involved in the progress of the Reformation; and we could imagine them, in company with several friends, John a Planitz, Jerome Schurff, Frederick Myconius, Justus Menius, Justus Jonas, Pomeranus, and Spalatin, not to mention others. They consulted upon the state of the churches; for these distinguished personages were appointed commissioners to fix suitable pastors in the different provinces of Saxony, and generally to superintend ecclesiastical affairs.

There is an interesting anecdote illustrative of the power of prayer, which may be appropriately associated with this very apartment.

"Melancthon, with Luther and other divines, met together for the purpose of consulting respecting the proper measures to be adopted in a certain exigency; and after having spent some time in prayer to Heaven, whence only they could expect adequate assistance, Melancthon was suddenly called out of the room, from which he retired under great depression of spirits. He saw during his absence some of the elders of the Reformed churches, with their parishioners and families. Several children were also brought hanging at the breast, while others a little older were engaged in prayer. This reminded him of the prophetic language, 'Out of the mouth of babes and sucklings hast Thou ordained strength, because of Thine enemies, that Thou mightest still the enemy and the avenger.' Animated by this interesting scene, he returned to his friends with a disencumbered mind and a cheerful countenance. Luther, astonished at this sudden change, said, 'What now! What has happened to you, Philip, that you are become so cheerful?' 'Oh, sirs,' replied Melancthon, 'Let us not be discouraged, for I have seen our noble protectors, and such as I will venture to say will prove invincible against every foe.' 'And pray,' returned Luther, thrilling with surprise and pleasure, 'who and where are these powerful heroes?' 'Oh,' said Melancthon, 'they are the wives of our parishioners, and their little children, whose prayers I have just witnessed—prayers which, I am satisfied, our God will hear: for, as our Heavenly Father and the Father of our Lord Jesus Christ has never despised or rejected our supplications, we have reason to trust that He will not in the present alarming crisis.'" [1]

It is worth while to add another instance of Luther's power in prayer, which occurred, not at Wittenberg, but at Weimar, where Melancthon, on his way to Hagenow, was lying ill. "When Luther arrived, he found Melancthon apparently dying. His eyes were dim, his understanding almost gone, his tongue faltering, his hearing imperfect, his countenance fallen, incapable of distinguishing any one, and indisposed to all nourishment. At such a sight Luther was in the most terrible consternation, and, turning to those who had accompanied him in his journey, exclaimed, 'Alas that the devil should have thus unstrung so fine an instrument!' Then, in a supplicating posture, he devoutly prayed, 'We implore Thee, O Lord our God, we cast all our burdens on Thee, and will cry till Thou hearest us, pleading all the promises which can be found in the Holy Scriptures respecting Thy hearing

---

[1] "Life of Melancthon," by Cox, p. 356.

prayer, so that Thou must indeed hear us, to preserve at all future periods our entire confidence in Thine own promises.' After this he seized hold of Melancthon's hand, and, well knowing the extreme anxiety of his mind, and the troubled state of his conscience, said, 'Be of good courage, Philip; you shall not die: although God has always a sufficient reason for removing us hence, He willeth not the death of a sinner, but rather that he should be converted and live. It is His delight to impart life, not to inflict death. God has received into His favour the greatest sinners that ever existed in the world, namely, Adam and Eve; much more will He not cast thee off, my dear Philip; or permit thee to perish in grief and guilt. Do not, therefore, give way to this miserable dejection, and destroy thyself; but trust in the Lord, who can remove it, and impart new life.' While he thus spake Melancthon began visibly to revive, as though his spirit came again, and was shortly restored to his usual health." [1]

Luther and Melancthon being so intimate, and both having families, it is natural to think of this Wittenberg room as having witnessed gatherings of the two households; Anne, Melancthon's eldest daughter, handsome and accomplished, of a literary turn— "the elegant daughter of Philip," as Luther politely calls her,— appearing as the flower of the flock. There would probably be Christmas-trees here, as at the neighbouring convent, and lute-playing, and childish sports, and clear, ringing laughter; nor can we help seeing amidst the group a certain servant of Philip Melancthon—one John, a staid, honest, faithful attendant, who figures in his master's biography as a sort of treasurer of the household, who skilfully managed the domestic expenses; an essential piece of service, for Philip seems no more than Martin to have excelled in the control of the exchequer. At the same time this faithful Eliezer-like retainer acted as tutor to the

---

[1] Seckendorf's Hist. lib. iii., p. 314. Cox relates it in his "Life of Melancthon, p. 421.

younger children; and thus gathering round himself so much of usefulness, and inspiring so much gratitude, when he came to die, after a service of thirty-four years, he was interred in the grave with honour, the members of the university being invited to his funeral, Melancthon delivering an oration and writing an epitaph.

At the back of Melancthon's house there is a garden, not kept in much order, but interesting from the preservation of a bower or alcove, with a stone table in it, said to have belonged to the Reformer. Here the two friends would sit at noon, or at eventide, under the shadow of the trees, engaged in consultation, no doubt with tankards of German beer foaming on the stone slab.

Differences between Luther and Melancthon respecting the eucharist and other theological subjects somewhat interrupted their confidential intimacy. Melancthon well knew Luther's temper and tendencies, and he remarked, "Often have I dreaded the old age of a nature so passionate." But the old flame of friendship revived in Luther before death terminated his earthly career, and he wrote affectionate epistles to Melancthon. What Melancthon thought of him when he was gone will be seen hereafter.

2. From the professor's house we pass to the artist's studio. The dwelling of Lucas Cranach, in Wittenberg, is one of the shrines whither travellers bent on seeing all that can be seen are likely to be conducted by the local cicerones. There were two artists of the name of Cranach—father and son,—both intimately connected with Martin Luther; and therefore the house in which they lived would be among his chosen haunts.

Lucas Cranach the elder was born in 1472, and died at Wittenberg in 1553. He was court painter to the three electoral princes—Frederick the Wise, John the Steadfast, and Frederick the Magnanimous; and in 1538 he became Burgomaster of the town. The marriage of Luther with Catherine von Bora is said to have been brought about mainly through the elder Cranach's assistance; and here we have at once a tie of love between the two families, which would often bring the Reformer with his wife and children over the artist's threshold. Luther had a taste for art, and so had Melancthon; and Cranach's pictures symbolical of the Reformation are spoken of by critics as "being worked out with the aid" of these two friends. Albert Dürer was appreciated by the three; but in Cranach the deep earnestness and grandeur of Dürer is "replaced by a simple and child-like serenity, and by a soft grace bordering almost on bashfulness." In Cranach's hands the imaginative element in art "produced some of its most fanciful and attractive results." Art had been abused and perverted in the Roman Catholic Church to superstitious ends of the worst type; but neither Luther nor Melancthon, on that account, wished to banish it from sacred service. They rather sought to bring it into connection with religious uses, such as might help forward the cause of the Reformation. Accordingly, we find pictures painted by Cranach, and still preserved in the Stadt Kirche, representing the rites of the Lutheran Church. There is the Last Supper, with the disciples seated round a circular table. There is Baptism, administered by Melancthon. There is Confession—for the practice of it, with certain modifications, at the time was allowed by Luther—with a portrait of Bugenhagen. There is a pulpit, with Luther preaching in front of a listening group of men and women and children. These pictures would be painted or prepared for in Cranach's studio; and as Luther figures so prominently in one of them, he would, in all probability, sit for his portrait to his friend, and he and Melancthon would give hints, suggestions, and criticisms as the work went on.

Lucas Cranach the younger, who followed his father in the burgomastership, and lived till the year 1586, based his style of painting on the study of his father and the study of Albert Dürer, and would not be likely in his after days to forget what in his youth he had heard from Luther in the old studio. In a chapel at the west end of the Stadt Kirche there is preserved a curious picture by this artist, representing the two ecclesiastical communities in Germany, in their relative position to each other. A vineyard appears, one half of which is being ruthlessly destroyed; priests are seen at work digging up plants and pulling things to pieces, whilst the other half is being carefully cultivated; the Reformers are seen as diligent husbandmen, planting, watering, and in all manner of ways improving the domain. We do not know the exact date of this work, whether or not it was executed in Luther's lifetime; but certainly it is a parable in canvas and paint, the design of which he would fully approve, and chuckle over with a hearty laugh.

3. From the house of Cranach we proceed to the castle, now the citadel, where dwelt the Electors of Saxony down to the year 1542. The three we have mentioned in connection with the elder Cranach all come into connection with this place, as they were all lords of the castle, and would there hold their courts, and keep high festival, with whatever of feudal state and splendour continued when the grand boundary line had been drawn between the age of mediævalism and the age of Reformation.

Frederick the Wise, founder of the University of Wittenberg—well styled "the hearthstone of the Reformation"—stood forth as Luther's protector at the Diet of Worms, and advised him not to leave the Wartburg; when Luther replied, in that dauntless style which he scrupled not to use towards princes as well as plebeians, " Since I now perceive that your electoral grace is very weak in faith, I can by no means regard your electoral highness as the man who is able to shield or save me." John the Steadfast, or Constant, succeeded his brother Frederick the Wise in 1525, joined Philip of Hesse in supporting the Reformation, united in the Protest at Spires, proclaimed the Confession at Augsburg, and died in 1532. "The straight line," he used to say, " is the shortest road ;" and such a man was likely to win Luther's heart. John Frederick the Magnanimous succeeded his father, John the Steadfast, and

FREDERICK OF SAXONY. BY ALBERT DÜRER.

established the Reformed doctrines within his territory in the year 1533. This Elector, a staunch Protestant, came under the ban of the empire in 1547, and was just afterwards defeated and made prisoner at Mühlberg, and at the same time condemned to death; a sentence commuted to deprivation of the electorate. He closed a troubled career in 1554. These three Saxon rulers were all friends of Luther, and welcomed him to the castle when they took up their residence in the town. One sees the shadow of the Reformer everywhere in the streets, especially near the old castle, of which the towers still remain. He enters before us, under the beetling brows of an archway, leading up to an inner palatial abode, glittering with the forms of men-at-arms and manifold other appurtenances of a German sovereign's court.

One visit which he paid—not, however, to converse with a friendly Elector, but to meet an emissary of the Pope—is made vivid in the pages of Sears' biography of the Reformer, where he is seen issuing from the university gate, and driving along the main street, accompanied by Bugenhagen, bound for the royal residence at the opposite end of the town.

"The papal legate Vergerio came, in this instance, to Wittenberg, to hold an interview with Luther himself, and the morning after his arrival invited Luther and Bugenhagen to breakfast. Early in the morning Luther sent for a barber to prepare him for the occasion, who, when he had come, said, 'How is it that you wish to be shaved so early?' 'I am to go,' replied Luther, 'to

---

[1] Sears' "Luther," p. 402. This amusing description is drawn from the account of Vergerio's visit given in "*Lutheri Opera*," tom. vi., p. 492. There is another account of the interview in Father Paul's "History of the Council of Trent," translated by Brent, p. 75, where Vergerio is represented as adopting a very conciliatory course, while Luther appears characteristically firm. A third account is given by Pallavicino, based on Vergerio's correspondence, which exhibits him as by no means friendly to the Reformer. Yet this account, like the other two, indicates Luther's decision, and his mistrust of any council which might be held. The interview, according to the Lutheran account, occurred on the 7th Nov., 1535.

the legate of his Holiness the Pope, and I must adorn myself so as to appear young; and the legate will then say to himself, "Is Luther so young, and yet hath done so much mischief? What, then, will he yet do?"' When his head was dressed, he put on his best clothes, and laid his jewel, set in gold, around his neck. The barber said to him, 'Doctor, that will be offensive to them.' 'For that reason I do it,' said Luther. 'They have conducted themselves offensively enough toward us; and we must manage in this way with those serpents and foxes.' 'Go, then, doctor,' said the barber, 'in God's name, and the Lord be with you, that you may convert them.' 'That,' said the doctor, 'I shall not do; but it may be that I shall read them a good lesson, and let them go.' He then mounted the carriage with Bugenhagen, and drove off to the castle to the legate. On the way he smiled and said to his companion, 'Here go the German Pope and Cardinal Bugenhagen; these are God's instruments and artillery.'

"On arriving at the place he was announced, and immediately admitted and kindly received, and he greeted the legate in turn, but not with the high-sounding titles which were formerly used on such occasions They soon began to speak of a council, and Luther said, 'You are not in earnest about holding a council; it is only a trick; and if you were to hold one, it would concern itself only about cowls, shorn heads, meats, drinks, and such-like foolish things, and others still more useless, which we know at the outset to be nothing. But of faith, and justification, and other useful and weighty matters, such as how believers may be united in spirit and in faith, you do not wish to confer, nor would it be for your interest. . . . But if you desire to have a council, very well: have one, and I will come, though I should know you would burn me at the stake.' 'Where?' answered the legate; 'in what city will you have the council?' 'Where you please,' was the answer. 'At Mantua, or Padua, or Florence, or wheresoever you please.' 'Will you come to Bologna'? said the legate. 'To whom does that place belong?' inquired Luther. 'To the Pope.' 'Gracious Lord! hath the Pope got his clutches on this city too? Well, I will come,' said Luther. The legate added, 'The Pope would not refuse to come to you at Wittenberg.' 'Well, then,' said Luther, 'let him come; we should like to see him.' 'How would you like to see him,' replied the legate,—'with an army or without?' 'Just as best pleaseth him,' said Luther; 'we will be ready for either.' Then the legate asked, 'Do you consecrate priests?' 'To be sure,' said Luther; 'for the Pope will not consecrate or ordain any for us. Here you see a bishop' (pointing to Bugenhagen) 'whom we have consecrated.' After the interview was over, and when the legate was seated upon his horse, he said to Luther, 'See that you are prepared for the council.' Luther replied, 'I will come, sir, with this neck of mine.'"

I must be allowed to add the name of another reformer, not a German, or a Swiss, but a Spaniard, who came on two occasions to reside in Wittenberg for a considerable time, and who must have had an intimate acquaintance with Melancthon, and probably with Luther also. His name was Franzisco de Enzinas—Enzinas signifying the ever-green oak. According to the fashion of the time, he translated his name into Greek, and called himself Dryander, as Schwarzerd, meaning black earth, called himself Melancthon. Enzinas was born at Burgos, but entered the university of Louvain in 1539, at that time under the domain of Charles V., King of Spain, as well as Emperor of Germany. Enzinas adopted reformed opinions, and became such an admirer of Melancthon that he said, "To enjoy the instruction of this man, I would travel to the very end of the civilised world." Accordingly he travelled to Wittenberg, and there entered himself, in October, 1541, as a student in the university, and became a resident in Melancthon's house. Melancthon was then in the zenith of his fame as the learned secretary of the Protestant Reformation, and Luther was leader and head of the Church in Saxony. The first

T

had written on theology, the second had translated the Word of God into German. Melancthon was admirably fitted to instruct the Spanish visitor in the principles of Protestant Divinity, and Luther would animate and guide him in another way. The heart of Enzinas was set on making a Spanish version of the Scriptures, and where could he meet with a better example and counsellor than the man who, as translator of the Bible, had fixed the language of his countrymen for ages to come? He profited by his Wittenberg residence, and returned to Louvain with a MS. of the New Testament in Spanish, which he submitted to the professors there. Securing an interview with the Emperor, he presented a printed copy of the work, soliciting his Majesty's patronage; but though favourably received by him at first, the Spanish Protestant was afterwards apprehended and imprisoned as a Lutheran and a friend of Melancthon.[1]

Thus we see in this instance what a mighty influence these two Germans possessed—how they gave a character to those who followed them, and what a heavy reproach and tremendous peril that character sometimes proved. To be the companion of Luther and Melancthon was to be a heretic, and, amongst Spaniards, to be liable to martyrdom by fire. Such a fate Enzinas narrowly escaped. In the middle of March, 1545, he was at Wittenberg once more, a guest in Melancthon's house, and probably enjoying further the friendship of Luther. "Our Spanish Franzisco is back, saved by Providence," says the former. He remained with his University friends till August, and then went to Leipzig. At the beginning of 1546 he returned to Wittenberg, about the time that Luther departed for Eisleben, there to die. The connection between this stranger from the south of the Pyrenees and the German theologians illustrates their far-spreading influence over Europe at that momentous era. No English, or French, or Swiss divines could in this respect be compared with

[1] I have given a full account of the interview between the Emperor and Enzinas in my book on the "Spanish Reformers."

TOWN HALL AND STADT KIRCHE, WITTENBERG.

them. In meditating upon the story of the Reformation in Spain and Italy, so far as it went in those countries, I am struck with the effect upon them, both of German books and German names. Translated, or in the original, the books made their way over the Pyrenees and over the Alps; and amongst the Spanish upper class there must have been many who could read German, if they could read at all, seeing that Charles v. held both Spain and Germany under his sovereign sway, and that his courtiers were composed of men taken from both lands. Certainly no voice rang through Europe in the sixteenth century like that of Martin Luther.

III. Luther's Work and Resting-place.

WITTENBERG contains two churches connected with the history of the great Saxon Reformer—the Stadt Kirche and the Schloss Kirche.

The Stadt Kirche stands in the middle of the town; and its double tower, surmounted by two smaller ones, resembling a couple of pepper-boxes, is welcomed by every one travelling in the neighbourhood as a conspicuous landmark; and by a visitor threading the thoroughfares of our Protestant Mecca, it becomes a sign pointing out the spot where the prophet of the Reformation fulfilled some of his most memorable ministries. The edifice is large and massive, externally plain, and without any architectural pretensions. The interior—commodious, and in Luther's time adapted to Protestant worship, as it still remains—affords little of interest beyond its associations.

Luther had no pastoral charge, his regular official duties being confined to the university. But he was an orator by nature, and a preacher by force of conviction; and therefore was drawn towards the pulpit as a sphere of activity. Not a mere rhetorician, he felt in his heart the thoughts which rushed through his mind. It was natural for him to utter in unstudied words the sentiments which moved his soul, even as a bird on the branch pours out its melodies by an instinctive impulse. He could not be silent: his constitution and habits did not fit him so much for commonplace details of ministerial work as for the special and eminently exceptional mission of a reformer of ancient abuses, and of a revivalist amidst more than ordinary formalism. Providence raised him up to overthrow accumulated superstitions; to rouse the population of Germany with the echoes of a voice from heaven; to awake the dead in trespasses and sins to a life of faith in the Redeemer; and to build up a reformed church, such as proved a blessed power in the land, and a glory and a joy for renovated Christendom to the ends of the earth. Luther was great as a university professor; great as an ecclesiastical administrator; great as a translator, commentator, and author; but greatest of all, for contemporary effects, as a preacher of God's Word.

His labours in this way covered a wide and varied field, and many an old German church may be pointed out as having rung with the sound of his voice; but some of the most remarkable memories of his oratory cluster round the pulpit of the Stadt Kirche—not the pulpit which stands there now, but one which occupied its place. Bugenhagen was pastor of this church in Luther's time; and in the years 1528 and 1529, when the pastor was performing missionary work in Brunswick and Hamburg, Luther preached, Sunday after Sunday, in his room. In 1530 and 1532, when Bugenhagen was similarly employed at Lubeck, Luther discharged homiletic duties three times a week—on Wednesdays, Saturdays, and Sundays. Again, between 1537 and 1540, when Bugenhagen was at work in Denmark, Luther upplied his place at Wittenberg. The sermons preached at this period, as Dr. Sears has observed, were not committed to paper by the preacher, but were written down by reporters; and these, after the lapse of three centuries, have been in part committed to the press. I may add that what are called his "Domestic Postils" were delivered at home to his own household, when he was so ill as to be unable to go to church. They connect themselves with the old room at the Augustinian monastery; and we can imagine the preacher, enfeebled by sickness, yet with eyes full of light and fervour, with a voice rising out of husky tones into sonorous utterances, and with an animated manner which reminded his hearers of earlier days, pouring out the gospel into the hearts of an auditory composed of wife, children, servants, neighbours, and friends. The scene reminds us of another—like it in spirit and manner—when Adolphe Monod, in Paris, just before his death, supported by pillows, gathered round the foot of his bed a domestic congregation, to which he addressed his loving adieux. I may further remark that Luther's "Church Postils" were prepared at the Wartburg for the use of the clergy, somewhat after the manner of the homilies of the English Church; so that from his castle height amidst the woods of Thuringia, there sounded out the word of the Lord, which floated from town to town, from village to village, from church to church, making glad the hearts of men, women, and children.

The Stadt Kirche is especially associated with a remarkable period in Luther's life. Whilst he was at the Wartburg, as we have seen, disturbances broke out at Wittenberg. Carlstadt, who figured at Leipzig, rushed into violent excesses during the Reformer's absence. After stimulating the people by fanatical discourses, he entered, at the head of a mob, into All Saints' Church at Wittenberg, and there began hewing down statues and pictures, with an iconoclastic fury perhaps rarely equalled, certainly never exceeded. As in other instances of popular tumult, the magistrates were panic-stricken, and the work of demolition went on in one church after another.[1] Nicholas Storch, in the

---

[1] In the Calendar of State Papers in the Record Office belonging to the period I observe the following:—" The head of the Church (Carlstadt) impugned the indulgence,

dress of a *Lanzknecht*, or free-lance trooper, and another man attired in a civic robe, were conspicuous leaders of the rabble; and after the news of these terrible proceedings had reached Luther in his retreat, he was at last induced to return to Wittenberg to appease the storm.

On reaching home the 7th of March, 1522, he writes to the Elector, "Satan has entered my fold, and committed ravages which my presence alone can repair. No letter can answer my purpose. I must interfere personally, and use my own eyes and my own mouth.

"My conscience will allow no longer delay; rather than act contrary to it I would incur the anger of your grace and of the whole world. The people of Wittenberg are my sheep, whom God has entrusted to my care. They are my children in Christ. I am ready to die for them. There can be no doubt whether I should come or not."

Luther, at the Wartburg, had allowed his beard to grow, and had laid aside his staff for a riding-whip. His monastic dress he exchanged for a steel cuirass, a plumed casque, and the spurred boots of a man-at-arms. Thus accoutred, he travelled homewards; and in a cloud of dust, "amidst a crowd of varlets," made his entry into Wittenberg, as represented in one of Cranach's pictures.

On the Sunday after his arrival, March 8, 1522, he appeared in the pulpit, and commenced a course of eight sermons on Charity, Christian Freedom (its use and abuses), Image-worship, Fasting, the Holy Communion, and Confession.

"Dear friends," he said (to adopt the translation by S. Winkworth), "the kingdom of God standeth not in speech or in words, but in power and in deed. For God will not have mere hearers

---

and proved by Holy Writ that the custom of vespers for the dead, and the indulgence likewise, were abuses and false. He threw down the money-box, and scattered its contents."—Dec. 31, anonymous.

and repeaters of the Word, but followers and doers of it, who exercise themselves in that faith which worketh by love. For faith without love is nothing worth: yea, it is not faith, but only a semblance thereof. Just as a countenance seen in a mirror is not a real countenance, but only a semblance thereof." No clearer testimony could be borne to the necessity of personal holiness; and therefore, whatever rash things Luther might at times utter with a view of glorifying the grace of God, he cannot be fairly charged with adopting Antinomian principles. He proceeded to urge prudence and caution upon his hearers in carrying out the work of Reformation, assuring them that with violence and uproar they would never do a Divine work. Not without effect did he appeal to the leaders of the outbreak. One of them when listening to him exclaimed, "It is as though I heard the voice of an angel, not of a man." Never, perhaps, was Virgil's description more signally verified, if we may take a liberty with the last line:

> "As when in tumults rise the ignoble crowd,
> Mad are their motions, and their tongues are loud;
> And stones and brands in rattling volleys fly,
> And all the rustic arms that fury can supply;
> If then some grave and pious man appear,
> They hush their noise, and lend a listening ear;
> He soothes with sober words their angry mood,
> And turns their evil passions into good."

Although there was an irresistible impulse moving Martin Luther to preach, at times the duty was a burden. One can understand this. The old Hebrew prophets felt it. So did St. Paul. The confession of it occurs in the writings and sayings of many a great preacher. Tauler, an object of admiration and a model of study for Luther, though a man of extraordinary eloquence, and making a mark in the history of mediæval preaching broader than that of any other divine, imposed on himself a season of silence, because of a mistaken consciousness of incompetency for the work to which he was called. It is the self-sufficient pedant, or the ignorant fanatic, who rushes into the pulpit without warrant or preparation. The true God-called preacher will tremble at the sight of the desk where he is to deliver his message, crying out, with apostolic humility, "Who is sufficient for these things?"

Accordingly, we find Luther saying, "Oh, how I trembled when I was ascending the pulpit for the first time! I would fain have excused myself, but they made me preach." "Here, under this very pear tree"—a pear tree in the monastery garden—"I have, over and over again, argued with Dr. Staupitz as to whether it was my vocation to preach. He said it was. I had fifteen reasons against it, and fifteen more when they were done. 'Doctor,' I used to say, 'you want to kill me. I shall not live three months if you compel me to go on.'"

Fear in the pulpit at the presence of certain men in the congregation is no uncommon thing, and Luther felt it at Wittenberg. "I don't at all like Philip to be present when I preach or lecture; but I make the best I can of it. I put the cross before me, and say to myself, Philip, Jonas, and the rest of them have nothing to do with the question in hand; and I try to persuade myself that I am as competent to fill the pulpit as they." Sometimes Luther, though a master of logic, was unmethodical in handling a subject, and became diffuse and unconnected, to the discomfort of his more learned listeners. Justus Jonas could not follow his friend's ramblings, and told him so, when Luther replied, he could not always follow them himself, regretting that he did not make his sermons shorter, and confessing that he was sometimes too wordy.

No man better knew himself; and few but will recognise the portrait which he draws of his own ministry, though they may not appreciate the force of the comparison which he institutes. Addressing Brentius, one of the Reformers, in a letter written August 26th, 1530, he observes, "My style is impracticable, harsh, rough; I pour forth a deluge, a chaos of words. My manner is turbulent, impetuous, fierce, like that of a gladiator contending with infinite monsters in uninterrupted succession. If one may compare small things with great, I should say there is given me somewhat of the fourfold spirit of Elias, who moved as the wind, and burnt like fire, and overthrew mountains, and burst rocks asunder. To you, on the contrary, is granted the gentle breeze which refreshes whatever it touches. One thing, however, consoles me, that the Divine Father of the human race needs for the instruction of His family both the one servant and the other—the rugged for the rugged, the harsh for the harsh. It is needful that God should not only irrigate in the rain, but also shake in the thunder, and purify in the lightning to render the earth more fertile."

But the freshness of Luther's imagination, the power of his feelings, his strong masculine sense, his affluence of speech, and his nationality of character, do not fully account for the effect of his ministry. He experienced the influence of the truth he proclaimed. Saved by the gospel, he preached it as the means by which others were to be saved. And with the spirit and style of the Holy Scriptures his mind and heart were so saturated, that his sermons were often translations and expansions of what he had read before ascending the pulpit. He had, as he said, " shaken every tree in this forest, and never without gathering some fruit."

All the men of the age, friends and foes, pronounced him the prince of preachers. " It was the preaching of Luther that endeared him to Frederick the Wise, even when he saw his own superstitions unsparingly exposed. It was his preaching that made him as absolute a ruler over the people at Wittenberg as Chrysostom was at Antioch and Constantinople, or Calvin at Geneva "—and, we may add, Knox at Edinburgh. " It was his preaching that so often stilled the tumult in the many towns and cities he visited during the first five years after his return from the Wartburg."

Near the Stadt Kirche, and close to the Rathhaus, is a Gothic canopy of cast iron, covering a bronze statue of the Reformer, executed by Schadow, and erected in the year 1822. On one side is written, in German, "If it be the work of God, it will endure; if of man, it will perish:" and on the other side, "A strong tower is our God." This structure occupies the site of a chapel, which was not removed until the walls became too decayed to stand any longer. It contained a pulpit made of planks, about a yard high, claiming an equal antiquity with the rude edifice in which it was placed. Here, according to tradition, the Reformer sometimes preached; and therefore at this spot another point of interest occurs to attract the notice of intelligent pilgrims to his homes and haunts.

But we must hasten on to the Schloss Kirche, or Castle Church at the end of the town opposite to that in which the Elster Gate and the Augustinian monastery are situated. It is much smaller than the church just left; but, on approaching it, the entrance arrests attention from the circumstance of its being connected with one of the boldest acts of Luther's life. The doors of the church at Milan were said to have been closed by St. Ambrose against the entrance of the Emperor Theodosius—significant of the courage of a renowned ecclesiastic in the maintenance of discipline. They occur to our recollection at the threshold of the Schloss Kirche, where the doors are significant of the courage of our Saxon Reformer in attacking the dogmas on which had long rested the reign of ecclesiastical despotism. Against them Luther affixed his ninety-five theses, now world-known—a challenge given to Papal Christendom—a gauntlet thrown down before the Romanized world.[1] It was in the autumn of 1517, on the eve of the Feast of All Saints, that Luther, agitated by the sale of indulgences, took certain counter-propositions, which he had elaborated with all the logical skill of the age, so as to cover the whole ground of the

[1] The theses were printed and widely circulated. I noticed one copy in the interesting Museum at Nuremberg.

controversy as he then apprehended it, and fastened the papers to the panel of the church gate. There it appeared before the public gaze. There it was read. There it was pondered. The proposition which serves as a key to the rest runs thus : " Every Christian who feels a true sorrow, a sincere repentance for his sins, has a plenary remission for his fault, even without an indulgence." Again : " The true and precious treasure of the Church is the holy gospel of the glory and grace of God." On that church threshold the public proceedings of the Reformation may be said to have begun. There sounded the trumpet-note which rolled over Germany from end to end.

As at Milan the old doors shut against Theodosius have vanished, so with the old doors to which Luther's theses were affixed. No fragment of the panelling even remains. The whole was burnt by the French ; the present gates are of bronze, from a design by Quast.

Most visitors to Wittenberg complain of the difficulty of gaining access to the Augustinian monastery and the Schloss Kirche, from the circumstance of the same person being custodian of the keys to both buildings. When we had surmounted the difficulty, and entered the church, we found ourselves in the presence of a worthy old German couple, who manifested a deep interest in the edifice and its memorials, and vied with each other in the office of cicerone. That interest was equalled only by the zeal of the old man in exhibiting photographs, facsimiles, and seal impressions—which form a staple of merchandise on this sacred spot—and the zeal of the old woman in providing for the comfort of her husband and lord. The hour of the mid-day meal having arrived, she showed an exemplary desire that the object of her affections should find refreshment amidst his toils ; and therefore, having sent him to his home to dine in quiet, she undertook his duties ; and, conducting us round the building, pointed out the several objects of interest which it contains. Here are the tombs of Frederick the Wise and John the Steadfast, both friends of the Reformer. The monument of Frederick is, as the guide-book says, "a fine work of art, by Peter Vischer, 1527 : his bronze statue is full of life, and of a noble character." The Gothic work of the niche is very beautiful.

But the two main objects are the graves of Martin Luther and Philip Melancthon. They are covered by tablets of bronze inserted in the stone pavement, and preserved by modern trap-doors opening over them. Two such graves are worth coming a long way to see ; and he who cares to take the journey for that purpose will scarcely fail to be moved in spirit, as he gazes on the last home of two who, in spite of transient jars, were lovely and pleasant in their lives, and in the tomb, rather than in death, not divided.

Standing over Luther's tomb, you recall the story of his death at Eisleben. He had arrived there on the 28th of January, 1546, and although very unwell, he took part in the conferences which ensued up to the 17th of February. He also preached four times, and revised the ecclesiastical regulations for the territory of Mansfeld. On the 17th he was so ill that the Counts entreated him not to quit his house. At supper, on the same day, he spoke a great deal about his approaching death ; and some one having asked him whether we should recognise one another in the next world, he said he thought we should. "I feel very weak," he exclaimed, "and my pains are worse than ever. If I could manage to sleep for half an hour, I think it would do me good." He did fall asleep, and remained in gentle slumber for an hour and a half. On awaking about eleven he asked, "What! are you still there? Will you not go and rest yourselves?" On their replying that they would remain, he began to cry with fervour, "'Into Thy hands I commend my spirit : Thou hast redeemed me, O Lord God of truth.' Pray, all of you, dear friends, for the gospel of our Lord ; pray that its reign may extend, for the Council of Trent and the Pope menace it round about." He then slumbered about an hour.

HOUSE WHERE LUTHER DIED, EISLEBEN.

When he awoke, he remarked, "I feel very ill. I think I shall remain here at Eisleben, here—where I was born." He walked about the room, and then lay down, and had a number of clothes and cushions placed over him to produce perspiration; but they had not the desired effect. "O my Father!" he went on to pray, "Thou, the God of our Lord Jesus Christ; Thou, the source of all consolation, I thank Thee for having revealed unto me Thy well-beloved Son, in whom I believe; whom I have preached and acknowledged, and made known; whom I have loved and celebrated, and whom the Pope and the impious persecute. I commend my soul to Thee, O my Lord Jesus Christ! I am about to quit this terrestrial body, I am about to be removed from this life; but I know that I shall abide eternally with Thee. 'Into Thy hands I commend my spirit: Thou hast redeemed me, O Lord God of truth.'" His eyes closed, and he fell back in a swoon. When he revived, Jonas said to him, "Reverend father, do you die firm in the faith you have taught?" He opened his eyes, looked fixedly, and replied, "Yes." Soon after, those nearest saw him grow paler and paler; he became cold; his breathing seemed more and more faint: at length, heaving one deep sigh, Martin Luther expired.

The corpse was brought to Wittenberg with much honour. In the procession, first came four deacons, then the officers of the Elector, on horseback; next the Counts of Mansfeld, with their attendants. The corpse followed in a leaden coffin covered with black velvet, on a funeral car. The widow (who was not with him when he died), in an open chariot, accompanied her husband's remains as chief mourner. The three sons, a brother, with his wife, and friends, two and two, including Philip Melancthon and Justus Jonas, brought up the rear.

The coffin being carried into the Schloss Kirche and placed on a bier in front of the altar, a funeral oration was pronounced by his friend Philip Melancthon. He remarked, "Often have

I myself gone to him unawares, and found him dissolved in tears and prayers for the Church of Christ. He devoted a certain portion of almost every day to the reading of the Psalms of David, with which he mingled his own supplications amidst sighs and tears; and he has frequently declared how indignant he felt against those who hastened over devotional exercises through sloth or the presence of other occupations. When a variety of great and important deliberations respecting public dangers have been pending, we have witnessed his prodigious vigour of mind, his fearless and unshaken courage. Faith was his sheet-anchor, and, by the help of God, he was resolved never to be driven from it."

A brass plate was fixed upon the grave, and still remains, bearing this inscription:—"Martini Lutheri, S. Theologiæ Doctoris Corpus H. L. S. E. qui anno Christi MDXLVI. XII. Cal. Martii Eyslebii in patria S. M. O. C. V. Ann. LXIII."

Charles V. entered Wittenberg after having besieged it, and expressed a wish to see the famous tomb. Reading the inscription with folded arms, he was asked by an attendant whether he would not have the grave opened and the ashes of the arch-heretic scattered to the winds. The Emperor's cheek grew red as he replied, "I war not with the dead. Let this place be respected."

There we leave our hero. We have traced him through many homes and haunts: we at last track his steps down to the eternal shores. "I die," said one of his countrymen, Jean Paul Richter, "without ever having seen the ocean, but the ocean of eternity I shall not fail to see." It is remarkable that in none of Luther's wanderings have we met with him by the sea-side. In towns and villages, amidst hills and valleys, in the depths of forests, on the banks of rivers, we find him walking, musing, working, but never on the margin of the mighty deep. On the waters of a main, broader and deeper than any of this world's, we have just beheld him embark, to find a haven and home in the land of the

THE EMPEROR CHARLES V.

After Titian, from a print in the British Museum.

blest. After the storms of life the words have been verified, as in that of many, many more, "Then are they glad, because they are at rest; and so He bringeth them unto the haven where they would be."[1]

There is scarcely time left for a visit to the Rathhaus of Wittenberg, a large building with long rows of windows opening from a plain wall, the deep roof being relieved by four large dormers, each with an ornamental facing, crowned by a fluttering vane. The steps of the main entrance were, when we visited the spot, crowded with the town authorities, celebrating the victory of Sedan. Flags were flying; bands of music were playing; trade was interrupted, and flocks of people had assembled in front of the town-hall to witness the proceedings in honour of such a proud occasion.

Besides pictures and other curiosities, including a portrait of Gustavus Adolphus, and a sword he left as a memorial of his visit to the Luther shrine, the Rathhaus contains the top of the Reformer's sacramental cup, and the rosary which he carried when he was a monk. It would be easy to draw up a long catalogue of relics, showing the veneration in which his name is held. There is an enormous difference between pretended and genuine remains, and between religious reverence paid to the former and natural interest taken in the latter. The mouldering bones of mediæval saints, exhibited in reliquaries within the sacristies of Roman Catholic churches, carry with them no proofs of genuineness, and in numerous cases must be of a spurious character; but such objects as are shown at Wittenberg and elsewhere in connection with Luther are such as, for the most part, carry along with them not only accredited traditions, but signs of credibility in their form and appearance. Were they brought out to receive religious honours, to have imprinted on them the kisses of devotees, such a practice would be opposed to the design and spirit of his whole

---

[1] I was much struck with this passage from the Psalms on a stone in the churchyard of Stratford-on-Avon—on the side next the grave of Shakspere.

career; but to preserve them as memorials, and to view them with interest is in accordance with feelings which it is impossible to suppress, and it would be absurd to condemn.

And here it may not be inappropriate to add that, besides personal relics, there exist numerous pictures, engravings, and medals of the Reformer. The pictures and engravings, hung on so many walls, or exhibited in so many windows, though varying considerably—some of them exhibiting a face worn away by ascetic practices, others a plump, cheerful German countenance,—generally agree in the essential form and features of the man. A photograph from a curious painting on wood, never published, which I met with at Strasburg, in one of my Luther pilgrimages, seemed at first to deviate from the common type, but on closer inspection one could recognise in the rather coarse portraiture his well-known image. Medals of him have been struck in abundance, and exhibit him in an immense variety of forms and associations. Now he appears as a tonsured priest, then in his cap and gown as a Wittenberg professor. In one case the reverse of his effigy presents an open Bible on the altar; in another, it exhibits an angel flying in the midst of heaven surrounded by the legend "Babylon the great is fallen, fallen!" The rose appears as his emblem; but more significantly and frequently the swan,— his favourite sign, as the reader will have already noticed,—in allusion to the story that John Huss said out of the goose, which his own name signified, would come a swan; this was applied to Luther. There is an instance in which he is seen standing with a book in one hand, a candle in the other, and under his feet the papal insignia, with a serpent wearing a triple crown. The swan is at Luther's side—and the surrounding words are, "*Magnus erat vita—major sermone—docendo maximus.*" His return from the Wartburg is celebrated by a representation of him bearded and wearing a cuirass on his breast; we also find on a medal of the Margrave of Brandenberg, the motto inscribed over the door of Luther's birthplace, "*Gottes wort und Luther's Lehr, wird vergehen nimmermehr,*" 1564. Luther and Huss, Luther and Melancthon, Luther and Catherine Bora, are combined together in some instances; and in a medal struck in 1546 he has his eyes shut, sleeping in death. Years afterwards, these mementos from the die of the engraver were renewed. They occur under the dates of 1617, 1630, 1670.[1]

I alluded just now to Luther's seal, of which impressions are sold at Wittenberg. It is a curious relic, full of symbolical significance. The seal is impressed upon red wax, and under it is a description of what Luther designed to represent by the figure it contains. The figure is that of a rose with a human heart inserted in the middle of the full-blown flower. The description refers to different colours, which of course could not be preserved in the embossed sealing-wax, but what they were appears from Luther's own account. It is given in a letter he wrote to Lazarus Spengler, and a translation from the German original runs as follows:—

"As you wish to know if my seal is successful, I will tell you the thoughts I wish to be embodied in it, as indicative of my theology. First of all there is a black cross in a heart presenting its natural colour, by which I intend to remind myself that we are saved by faith in the crucified One. If we believe with the heart we are justified. Through it runs a *black* cross, because the cross mortifies and gives pain. At the same time it leaves the heart in its original colour. It does not destroy natural affection. It does not kill, but keep alive; for the just *lives* by his faith—faith in the crucified One. But this heart must be put in the middle of a *white* rose, to show that faith gives peace, consolation, joy. The rose is *white*, not red, because white is the colour of spirits and

[1] These details are taken from a curious book, entitled, " *Vita D. Martini Lutheri, &c., nummis CXLV et Iconibus, aliquot varissimis, confirmata et illustrata, &c.*, studio M. Christiani Juncker. MDCXCIX."

angels. This rose is amidst a field of heavenly *blue*, for spiritual joy and faith are the beginning of future bliss, which is already embraced by hope, though not fully manifested. Round the *blue* field is a *golden* ring, to show that bliss in Heaven lasts for ever, having no end, and is glorious above all things, even as gold is the most precious of metals."

Luther used to say about his seal, that the heart of the Christian rests on roses, whilst it stands underneath the cross.

> "The Christian heart a rose-strewn pathway treads,
> When o'er his way the cross a radiance sheds."

All this is characteristic of the man. We see in it his vivid imagination, the mystic element which pervaded his evangelical thoughts, and, especially, the bright and beautiful piety which shone over his whole life.

The memory of Luther is engraven upon the town of Wittenberg more indelibly than any other. Even the reputation of Philip Melancthon pales in connection with the lustre of his colleague's fame. The fortunes of war, which have thrown shadows over the town—such as the Austrian bombardment in 1760, when one-third of the buildings were destroyed, and the Prussian siege in 1814, when the place was taken by storm—are events scarcely remembered by readers of history as they walk through the streets. But everybody, on approaching the gates, thinks of the Saxon monk who there lived and there lies buried. Washington Irving concludes his essay on "Shakspere and Stratford-on-Avon" by remarking that it would have cheered "the spirit of the youthful bard that his name should become the glory of his native place, that his ashes should be religiously guarded as its most precious treasure, and that its lessening spire, on which his eyes were fixed in tearful contemplation, should one day become the beacon towering amidst the gentle landscape, to guide the literary pilgrim of every nation to his tomb." It is no depreciation of

Shakspere's genius to say, that above his aspirations after fame, whatever they might be, rose the aims and desires of Luther—a man absorbed in zeal for the salvation of souls, and for the glory of his Saviour ; but it would have filled him with wonder—perhaps given him pleasure—could he have foreseen the place he was to occupy in the history of the world, and how the double tower of the Stadt Kirche, in which he preached, would become a beacon to guide tens of thousands from both hemispheres to the Augustinian monastery, where he lived, and to the Schloss Kirche, where he lies entombed.

INDEX.

Aleander, *page* 128
Alexis, 48
Altenburg, 166, 228
Altenstein, 139
Amsdorf, Nicholas, 35
Auerbach, 96
Augsburg, 81; arrival of Luther at, 83; palace, 84; St. Anna Church, 85; Luther's departure, 89; Frauen Thor, 89; Diet, 90; Confession, 91
Augustinian monastery at Erfurt, 44; at Wittenberg, 240

Basle, description, 76; time of Luther's visit, 77
Bible, 47; various editions, 48, 248; Latin, 229; Luther's translation, 245
Bologna, Luther's illness, 61
Brunswick, Erick, Duke of, 127
Bugenhagen, 271
Bucer, Martin, 72
Bulls, Papal, burnt by Luther, 249

Cajetan, Cardinal, 83, 88
Carlstadt, 99; arrival at Leipzig, 101; conference with Luther, 171
Catacombs at Rome, 65
Catherine von Bora, Letters to her from Luther, 17, 191, 237; marriage, 250
Coburg, 71; castle, 213
Confession of Augsburg, 91; of Schmalkalden, 218
Contarini, Gaspar, Letters of, 128, 143
Corpus Christi Day, 20

Cotta, Conrad, 31
Cotta, Frau Ursula, 31
Cranach, Lucas, the elder, 266
Cranach, Lucas, the younger, 267

D'Aubigné, Merle, 36
D'Enzinas, Franzisco, 273; translation of New Testament, 274
Diet of Augsburg, 90; of Worms, 113
Döllinger quoted, 247
Dürer, Albert, 195

Eck, Dr., 99; arrival at Leipzig, 101
Ehrenburg, 213
Eisleben, description, 5; birthplace of Luther, 8; church of St. Peter, 14; church of St. Andrew, 15; gymnasium, 20
Eisenach, description, 25; Nicolaithurm, 25; St. George's Church, 26; Luther's sermon, 35; parochial school, 26; house of Ursula Cotta, 31; school-house, 32; Luther's visits, 32, 35; centenary jubilee, 36
Elizabeth of Hungary, 137; grave, 178
Erfurt, history, 40; description, 43; Augustinian monastery, 44; Martinsstift, 51; Luther's reception, 58; Luther's sermon, 59; fanaticism, 169; Luther revisits, 169

Florence, Luther's visit, 62
Francke, A. H., 232
Frankfort, 35; Luther's house, 116
Franz of Sickengen, 115
Frederick the Wise, 268

INDEX.

Friars, rivalry amongst, 53

George of Freundsberg, 125

Halle, history, 231; Luther's lodgings, 235
Harz scenery, 5
Heidelberg, Luther visits, 61; description, 68; *Wolfsbrunnen*, 68; *Königstuhl*, 68; castle, 68; conference, 72; university: early Bibles, 78
Hund, Knight von, 140
Hutten, Ulric von, Letter, 123

Indulgences, 202

Jena, 171; narrow escape of Luther, 172, 174
John Frederick the Magnanimous, 268
John the Steadfast, 268
Jonas, Justus, 185
Judenbach, Luther's visit, 200
"Junker Georg," 36, 155

Kessler, of St. Gall, 156
Königstuhl, 68

Leipzig, 95; Auerbach's cellar, 96; castle of Pleissenburg, 96; debate, 100; Luther's sermon, 106; Nicholas Church, 108
Leuchtenberg, Castle of, 106
Loyola, Ignatius, 31
Lutherbaum, 117
Luther, Elizabeth, 257
Luther, Hans, 7; portrait, 14; discipline, 26; poverty, 27; death, 257
Luther, Magdalene, death, 257
Luther, Margaret, portrait, 14
LUTHER, MARTIN:—
  Anecdotes of, 7, 156, 249, 262, 263, 265, 271
  Bible, 32; discovery of one, 47; translation, 245
  Birthplace, 8
  Burial, 289
  Burns the Pope's Bull, 248
  Capture, 140

Contest with the devil, 150
Conversational power, 260
Death, 19, 286
Description by Bucer, 72; at Leipzig, 102
Education, 14
Education, zeal for, 21
Farewell to his friends, 51
House where he died, 16
Hymn, 120, 121, 215
Illness, 35; on his journey to Rome, 62; at Schmalkalden, 228
Interview with Vergerio, 271
Itinerary, 174
Last sermon, 16
Letters to his wife, 17, 191, 237; to Spalatin, 73, 90, 105, 140, 256; to Melanchthon, 84, 92, 154, 216; to Cuspianus, 125; to Frederick Myconius, 175; to Justus Jonas, 217; to Amsdorf, 235; to Chancellor Rühel, 253; to his son, 256; to the Elector, 280
Marriage, 250
Monk, becomes a, 44
Monument at Worms, 131
Music, love of, 259
Novitiate, 51
Portraits, 8, 15, 51, 85, 149, 262
Prayer at Worms, 122; for Melancthon, 264
Priesthood, enters the, 54
Relics, 8, 13, 51, 150, 230, 293
Theses, 72
Trial, by Cardinal Cajetan, 85
Work, 277
Luther's seal, description, 295

Mansfeld, Counts of, 6; quarrels between 18; peace restored by Luther, 18
Mansfeld lakes, 5; Luther's removal to the town, 14
Marburg, 177; meeting of Luther and Zwingli, 182; Knights' Hall, 185
Martinsstift, 51
Mathesius quoted, 47, 122, 246

INDEX.

Melancthon, Anne, 265
Melancthon, portraits, 8, 15; relics, 13; bust, 15; friendship for Luther, 265; grave, 286
Milan, 61
Mühlhausen, 173
Munich, 61
Münzer, Thomas, 165, 177

Neuenheim, 74
Nesselwang, 161; castle of Hohenschwangen, 161
Nicolaithurm, 25
Nördhausen, 174
Nuremberg, 194

Œcolampadius, 185
Oemler, Nicholas, 15
Oppenheim, 113
Orio, Lorenzo, Letter of, 175
Orlamünde, 174

Pantheon, 62
Pavia, Luther's illness, 61
Peasant Wars, 170
Pfiffligheim, 113, 117
Philip the Magnanimous, 181, 192
Philip II., 242
Pilate's Staircase, 66
Pleissenburg, Castle of, 96; debate, 100
Peasants, Grievances, 172

Reformation, Centenary jubilee at Eisenach, 36
Reinicke, Hans, 15
Rome, Cause of Luther's journey, 61; description, 62; Luther's impressions of, 62; Pantheon, 62; Catacombs, 65; St. Peter's, 66; Pilate's Staircase, 66; St. John Lateran, 66
Rosengarten, Island of, 109

Sannersche Haus, Schmalkalden, 223

Saxe-Weimar, Library, 1
Schmalkalden, 218; Luther's lodgings, 223; confession, 224; church, 228
Schmalkalden, League of, 221
Schweina, Extract from parish records, 144
Seeburg, 173, 175
Sonneberg, description, 18; Luther's house, 200; festival, 205
Staupitz, 20; conversation with Luther, 53
Stolberg, 174
Storch, Nicholas, 165
Stotterheim, 48
Swabia, description, 160; its people, 163

Tauler, 281
Thüringerwald, 155
Trebonius, 27
Tyndale, William, 192; interview with Luther, 247

Vergerio, 271
Völkerschlacht, 99

Wartburg, Castle of, 36; description, 136; history, 144; chapel, 149; Ritterhau, 149
Weimar, 175
Weissenfels, 71
Wittenberg, 61; description, 238; university, 239, Augustinian monastery, 240; Luther's study, 242; Stadt Kirche, 277; Schloss Kirche, 277; Luther's Sermon, 279
Wolfsbrunnen, 68
Wonnegau, 109
Worms, description, 109; Diet, 113; Luther's approach, 113; Bishop's Hof, 124; Luther at Diet, 125; Luther's monument, 131; Bible stand, 131; cathedral, 135
Würzburg, 71

Zwickau, 165; Luther's sermon, 166
Zwingli, 181; prayer, 191

www.ingramcontent.com/pod-product-compliance
Lightning Source LLC
Chambersburg PA
CBHW022058230426
43672CB00008B/1212